CONTENTS

Fishing on Lake Erie

day 47/100

Welcome

THIS BOOK IS FOR YOU.

WHO ARE YOU?

I started writing this book with the intention of focusing on "newcomers" to Cleveland – as a relocation guide for people who wanted an urban experience in Northeast Ohio. But I think it will also interest people who already live here, because it provides a tool for discovering or rediscovering the city.

You could be just about anyone who wants to learn more about the City of Cleveland. Maybe you're outside the region completely, and are considering a move here. Maybe for a job, or for school, or because you're looking for a new start and considering your options.

Maybe you already live here and want to learn more. Maybe you live in the suburbs but you've thought of moving closer into town someday. Or you're staying put in the suburbs, but you want to a guide to exploring the city.

I've divided the book into two basic sections. In the first, I try to shed some light on what it's like to live in Cleveland. In the second, I provide the facts on individual neighborhoods, so you can explore them for yourself.

I've done my best to be honest. I don't work for the chamber of commerce, and my job isn't to persuade you that Cleveland is perfect. Cleveland offers incredible opportunities, and I don't downplay those. At the same time, Cleveland has problems, and I try not to sugarcoat them. I hope you will get a realistic picture of Cleveland, in all its complexity, from reading this book.

This is not a conventional guide to Cleveland. It's not an attempt to provide an exhaustive overview of the entire region. It doesn't even provide an exhaustive overview of the entire city. Instead, I've chosen to focus on neighborhoods that I think provide the best "points of entry" for people who want an active, urban lifestyle.

Although I've tried to write with an eye to all types of potential residents and visitors to Cleveland – women, immigrants, people of various races – I'm sure that my own background and upbringing factor into what I've chosen to feature. Rather than fight that too hard, I've decided to offer what I know. As you continue to research the city, you'll hear from other people from other backgrounds – and that's great. The more people you talk to, the more you'll learn about all Cleveland has to offer.

In short, this book is for people who are looking at Cleveland with fresh eyes, or who want to look at Cleveland with fresh eyes. People, in short, who are New to Cleveland.

Again, welcome. There's a lot to see.

A Note on the Illustrations

A few months ago, a friend told me about a blog called 100 Days in Cleveland. The author of the blog, illustrator and designer Julia Kuo, set a goal for herself of posting a new drawing every day, for 100 days, of something she loved in Cleveland. Like many other people, I was captivated by Julia's drawings – not only because of their beauty, but because of the way they made me see my city in a new way. Some of the things she drew I hadn't known about; others I had, but had never appreciated them properly.

When I was finishing up this book, I contacted Julia to ask if I could use some of her drawings in my book. After a few weeks of talking, Julia asked if I would be open to making the book a full-scale collaboration: my text with her drawings. My response was something like, "Wow. Um, yes!!!" I feel so fortunate to have met Julia, and to have her work included here. You'll notice that the drawings have numbers on them; these are the days on which Julia originally drew them.

Our teaming up is an example of the kind of creative synergy that I've encountered so often in Cleveland since I moved back in 2005. This is an exciting time for the city, a time of reinvention and creativity. It only takes a little curiosity – and a willingness to talk to strangers! – to tap into that energy.

The Cultural Gardens in University Circle

day 46/100

INTRODUCTION & BASICS

In 2005, The New York Times ran an article about Cleveland in its "36 Hours" travel series. The story glowed with praise about the city. "There's a thriving art scene in Tremont," it reported, "and the retooled Warehouse District has become a place to be, rather than flee, after dark. Clevelanders remain, by nature, a self-deprecating lot. But before long, calling their town hip, cosmopolitan – even splendid – won't sound so ironic."

The paper returned in 2009, and the dispatch was even more laudatory: "Instead of abandoning the city, local entrepreneurs and bohemian dreamers alike are sinking roots; opening a wave of funky boutiques, offbeat art galleries and sophisticated restaurants; and injecting fresh life into previously rusted-out spaces."

Then, a year later, Forbes.com offered a rather – ahem – different take. It placed Cleveland at the top of its third annual survey of "The Most Miserable Cities in the U.S." Not much had improved in Cleveland, the article said, since the infamous Cuyahoga River fire in 1969. Forty years on, misery continued to reign due to "high unemployment, high taxes, lousy weather, corruption by public officials and crummy sports teams."

So which publication is right? Well, both contain kernels of truth. Cleveland is a city of contradictions.

On the one hand, a new spirit of entrepreneurship seems to be taking hold, with people of all ages opening stores and businesses. You need only stroll W. 25th Street in Ohio City to see evidence. On the other, the high school graduation rate in the city proper is just 54 percent, and too many families – as many as a third of the city's households – live below the federal poverty line. Meanwhile, the city's population continues to decline (to just under 400,000, according to the 2010 Census – less than half the 1950 peak).

On the one hand, start-up technology companies have been moving into office space in Downtown, Midtown and University Circle, signaling blue-collar Cleveland's transition to a more diversified, knowledge-based economy. On the other, manufacturing jobs – long the region's economic bedrock – have continued to dwindle.

The list goes on.

These paradoxes have given Clevelanders a complicated psychology. Many are fiercely devoted to their city even as they outwardly denigrate it – probably a defensive move, meant to deflect others from making fun first.

The truth is, there are countless reasons to love Cleveland – and you'll learn about many of them on the following pages. The city has the same cultural amenities as cities two or three times its size, but the cost of living is a pittance in comparison. If you're an entrepreneur or an artist, Cleveland's low overhead as you establish yourself can more than make up for any perceived deficits. The low cost of living is also a boon for young families and retirees on fixed incomes.

Many people move to more prosperous cities because they want something from them: a high-paying job, active nightlife, culture, cool friends. What those cities sometimes lack, though, are opportunities to give back. They're already doing fine.

In Cleveland, citizens' contributions to the city are greatly valued. Whether you attend public meetings to advocate for more open government or open a new store or start a new business, you'll likely be contributing something wanted and welcome.

So why does Cleveland's reputation suffer? A big reason may be that the city strikes out on several conventional, growth-oriented measures of success – the things that we, as affluent Westerners, are taught to value from an early age. The local economy is stagnant. The population is flat or falling. Home values are low.

To live in Cleveland is in some ways an endorsement of a different set of values: a kind of DIY, community-oriented ethos that's not too concerned with what the coasts think. Living in Cleveland is a bit nonconformist. (Fun, right?)

BRIEF HISTORY

The area that's now Cleveland was once part of a huge ocean that covered most of the interior of the United States. Creatures like the Dunkleosteus – a huge shark-like monster with sharp teeth – swam here, and you can view their fossilized remains in the Cleveland Museum of Natural History.

After the ocean dried up, the Ice Age arrived and glaciers smoothed out the land. The glaciers left behind Lake Erie and fertile soil that supported a dense deciduous forest.

People started living in the area around 10,000 years ago. Many Native American tribes lived in or traveled through the area, including the Iroquois, Erie, Chippewa and Ottawa. One of the sites thought to be sacred to the Indians was a large, blue clay mound on the west side of the mouth of the Cuyahoga River, near what's now Downtown Cleveland ("Cuyahoga" itself is an Algonquinian word meaning "crooked river"). Most early white-people maps of Cleveland show the mound, but it disappeared in the 19th century, probably bulldozed for industry.

A scattering of white people, mostly French fur trappers, came through in the 17th and 18th centuries. Other than that, life was pretty quiet until 1796, when Moses Cleaveland arrived from Connecticut to survey property in the so-called Western Reserve – a slice of Northeast Ohio that Connecticut had claimed in the mid-18th century.

Cleaveland surveyed the area around the mouth of the Cuyahoga River and the land was opened for settlement. The town of Cleveland (the "a" eventually disappeared) was born. The first permanent settler was Lorenzo Carter, who arrived in 1797. He opened the city's first tavern and eventually established a farm on what's now called Whiskey Island, just west of the Cuyahoga River, in the first years of the 19th century. A distillery was built there in the 1830s, giving the Island its colorful name. Whiskey Island – in fact a peninsula – is today home to Wendy Park, a water treatment plant and a couple of industries.

Cleveland remained a weak draw for the first decades of the 19th century. The town, and Whiskey Island in particular, was a haven for mosquitoes because of the abundance of water. Cholera and malaria felled a number of early settlers.

In the days before railroads and highways, though, that abundance of water was also Cleveland's main asset. By the 1820s, tycoons of business and industry had funded construction of a new shipping canal from the Ohio River in Portsmouth to Lake Erie in Cleveland. It opened up trade routes to both the St. Lawrence Seaway and the Erie Canal through upstate New York. Cleveland was on its way, becoming a trading hub for agricultural goods.

At first, the mouth of the river was the site of twin cities – Cleveland and Ohio City. Cleveland was on the east side of the river, Ohio City on the west. The canal helped both places grow. Some of the small brick cottages in what's now the Ohio City neighborhood of Cleveland date from the canal days. There was strong rivalry between the two cities. The most famous example of this was the so-called Bridge War, when Ohio City vigilantes – perhaps drunk on spirits from Whiskey Island – set off explosives on a Cleveland-funded bridge across the Cuyahoga River. Cleveland annexed Ohio City in 1854, though the division between east and west is far from forgotten. Debates about which side of town is "better" still rage in contemporary Cleveland. To participate in these debates is a favorite – though wearying – method of showing one's Cleveland-ness. It's sort of like complaining about winter or the Cleveland Browns (p. 19).

Cleveland remained a transportation hub in the railroad era, beginning in the 1850s or so. There were a few reasons for this. One, the city was a convenient gateway from the Northeast to the Midwest and West. You practically had to come through Cleveland to get from Boston or New York to Chicago, for example, and points west. Two, Cleveland lay between the iron ore fields of Minnesota and the coal fields of southern Ohio and Pennsylvania. Steel mills sprang up in the Cuyahoga Valley south of downtown Cleveland to process the tons of ore and coal that arrived by train. A couple mills are still there, including a large plant owned by Luxembourg-based steel giant Arcelor Mittal. The smokestacks – best viewed from I-490 – belch soot and shoot flame like something out of Dickens. Imagine this sight times 20, and you get an idea of how Cleveland must have looked (and smelled) in the heyday of the American steel industry from 1880 to 1950.

Industry begat industry, and by the 1910s Cleveland was one of the manufacturing giants of the world. Steel was big, but so were textiles and – later – automobile parts. People came in droves for jobs. The early 1900s saw an influx of Eastern European immigrants – from places like Italy, Hungary, Czechoslovakia, Slovenia and Poland – who defined Cleveland's culture for most of the century. In 1920 the city was the fifth largest in the country, behind New York, Chicago, Philadelphia and Detroit. Well-paying, unionized factory jobs seemed to grow on the city's many trees (one of Cleveland's nicknames is "Forest City").

The housing paradigm in older East Coast cities had been small apartments and rowhouses. But in Cleveland, middle-class families could afford to own single-family houses. The idea of a garden and white-picket fence, and walls separate from one's neighbors, helped attract thousands. It also helps explain why Cleveland today is predominantly a city of single-family detached homes (see p. 26).

Names synonymous with greed and cigars – John D. Rockefeller, Andrew Carnegie, Marcus Hanna – made their fortunes here. Rockefeller, who became the richest man in the world at the turn of the 20th century – looms especially large in the local imagination. Cofounder of Standard Oil, he lived in a mansion on Euclid Avenue near downtown and then – setting a trend that continues to this day among Cleveland's old-money elite – built a larger estate on the far East Side, in what's now East Cleveland. That estate, Forest Hill, is now a lovely if frayed park. The availability of land and a lack of natural barriers like mountains continues to fuel sprawl in Northeast Ohio.

Cleveland continued to simmer as an industrial powerhouse through the first half of the 20th century. But internal tensions were beginning to build, particularly around race. African Americans had been emigrating to Cleveland from the South since the 19th century for factory jobs. The years after World War II saw an increased number making the journey north. They settled mostly on the city's east side, in established black neighborhoods like Central and Hough. Those neighborhoods soon became overcrowded.

This led to two negative outcomes that in hindsight seem utterly predictable. First, African American residents in older black neighborhoods like Hough became frustrated by overcrowding and racist attitudes that seemed to demand they stay put. Second, white residents in the neighborhoods where blacks were now moving – such as the Jewish enclave of Glenville – felt threatened and left for the suburbs ("white flight").

The urban renewal movement of the 1950s and 1960s fanned the flames of these tensions. City leaders approved demolition of large swaths of "problematic" neighborhoods – especially Hough and Central – to make way for public housing projects, highways and unidentified "future development opportunities" (in many cases, the sites are still vacant). Displacement of those neighborhoods' residents caused further tension in the white neighborhoods where they relocated. As in other cities, urban renewal in Cleveland started a cycle of demolition, relocation, white flight and abandonment that now stretches to the suburbs and has yet to reach a clear end.

The high water mark of white-black tension came in the late 1960s, when riots broke out in both Hough and Glenville. Blacks were protesting poor housing conditions, discrimination by landlords and mortgage lenders and mistreatment by white police. The riots, like Rockefeller's abandonment of the city, left a deep scar on the city's psyche. Although race relations have improved since the 1960s, distrust between blacks and whites is still palpable in Cleveland. There are often clear boundaries between "white" and "black" neighborhoods in both the city and the suburbs.

Cleveland endured another infamous trauma in 1969, when an oil slick on the Cuyahoga River caught fire. In fact, the river had burned about a dozen times before, dating back to 1868, and the 1969 fire was comparatively minor. Cleveland wasn't the only city to have a burning river. Fires had also broken out on waterways in Philadelphia, Buffalo and Chicago. But by the late 1960s, national awareness of the environment had heightened, and the Cuyahoga fire became a symbol of industry's befouling of nature.

Guardian of Traffic
Built in 1932
day 88/100

Attention to the incident led Congress to pass the Clean Water Act in 1970. But the negative press for the city was torrential, inspiring disgusted newspaper editorials and much mockery among late night TV hosts. (In fact, the burning river jokes continue to this day – though they are probably less frequent than many Clevelanders think.) Today, the river is cleaner than it's been in decades and biologists have reported signs of ecological renewal. Since the 1990s, there have been countless – and sometimes clumsy – examples of local businesses and citizens trying to reclaim and invert the burning river identity into a source of pride. Great Lakes Brewing Company (see p. 88), for example, bottles a Burning River Pale Ale and runs the annual Burning River Festival, focused on environmental themes. The local women's roller derby team calls itself the Burning River Roller Girls.

Further bad press came in 1978, when Cleveland, under then-mayor Dennis Kucinich (yes, *that* Dennis Kucinich – now a U.S. Representative and frequent far-left presidential candidate), defaulted on loans from six local banks. It was the first major American city since the Depression to do so, though New York had come close a few years earlier.

Cleveland's story since then has been similar to that of a recent college graduate – lots of soul-searching and exploration and tentative attempts at self-reinvention. There's a sense of both uncertainty and possibility in the air.

Some conventional markers of success look gloomy. The population as of the 2010 Census had fallen to 398,000 – the lowest number since 1900. Factories have closed or relocated abroad or to the South. The median household income in the city proper is about $25,000, and about a third of households are below the poverty line. Perhaps most troubling, the city continues to be among the most racially segregated in the country, according to an analysis of 2010 Census data by Salon.com. Although Cleveland fares no worse than cities such as New York and Chicago in this respect, it has a long way to go to overcome the racial tension of the last 100 years.

But there are many signs of a new city taking shape. Amid bad economic news nationwide, The Brookings Institution and the London School of Economics reported in 2010 that Cleveland was experiencing the 10th-strongest recovery of any large metro area in the nation. Small startups are leasing some of the empty office space downtown and in hulking former factories like Tyler Village in Asiatown. There has been a small and welcome boom in artisan businesses, specializing in everything from bicycle repair to ice cream. In 2010 the restaurant scene was named one of the best in the nation by The Chicago Tribune, and new palaces du cuisine seem to open every month.

Downtown Cleveland has a fast-growing residential population, with former office buildings and warehouses being converted to apartments. Neighborhoods like Tremont, Ohio City, Asiatown, University Circle and Detroit-Shoreway are in various stages of rebirth, with immigrants and younger residents moving into bargain Victorian houses. Between 2005 and 2009, the number of 25- to 34-year-old, college-educated adults living within 3 miles of downtown increased 49 percent, according to CEOs for Cities. Downtown Cleveland's apartment occupancy rate is 95 percent. Outsiders are taking note. In 2007, The Economist named Cleveland the "most livable" city in the U.S. (in a tie with its neighbor Pittsburgh).

EXPECT THE UNEXPECTED

Newcomers arriving in Cleveland from "cooler" or newer cities are typically surprised by a few things – some positive, some negative. Let's start with the positive.

1. Housing is sooo inexpensive.
It's true. You can buy a big house, ready to be occupied, for well under $200,000 even in "cool" neighborhoods. That amount won't even buy you a closet in New York or San Francisco. Rental rates, meanwhile, hover around $500 for a nice one-bedroom and $700 for a two-bedroom, with even better deals available in less-established areas.

2. The arts and culture are great.
Cleveland has some of the most respected high-art institutions in the country, including the Cleveland Orchestra and the Cleveland Museum of Art. It has an international piano competition, a cinematheque and an international film festival. But probably in large part because of the low cost of living, it also has an increasingly vibrant underground and independent art scene. Galleries abound in Tremont and Asiatown, and lanky-haired rockers patrol the sidewalks of North Collinwood and Lakewood, awaiting their next gigs at the Beachland Ballroom or the Grog Shop (For more on arts and culture, see p. 210).

3. There's, like, no traffic!
People from bigger cities, especially those on the coasts, will be amazed at how little traffic they have to battle to get around by car. Even at rush hour, you're unlikely to experience more than a few minutes' delay.

4. Lake Erie looks as big as an ocean.

Amazing, isn't it? You can even surf on it (p. 150). Cleveland hasn't had the best track record of connecting residents to Lake Erie, but the political will for better access is building. In the meantime, neighborhoods like North Collinwood, Detroit Shoreway, Edgewater and Lakewood already have easy waterfront access.

5. It's close to a lot of other places.

Washington, D.C., Toronto and Chicago are six hours away by car. New York City is eight or nine. Pittsburgh is two. (See p. 23)

6. People are so nice here. (But see also #9)

A lot of transplants – especially from the coasts – find Clevelanders to be warm and welcoming. Many are surprised that strangers on the sidewalks smile or say hello. They may find cab drivers or cashiers friendlier than their coastal counterparts.

7. There's a lot going on! Almost too much at times.

The corollary to Cleveland's quiet winters (see #12) are its action-packed springs, summers and falls. If you can't find at least five things to do on a Friday or Saturday night between April and December, you're not looking hard enough. Or at all.

Now on to the negatives.

8. Everyone drives. Everywhere.

Well, not everyone. But most, yes. For the last 50 years, Cleveland – and to an even greater extent Ohio – has chosen to sprawl rather than become denser. We have invested more in highways than in transit or bicycling infrastructure. Racial tension and permissive land use laws have fueled an exodus to far flung suburbs not only by people but businesses. To visit friends and get to work, people drive 20, 30, even 50 miles a day. All that said, Cleveland is a lot more walkable and transit-friendly than most cities in the South and West, and the city has begun to signal a greater openness to alternative transportation (p. 202).

9. A lot of the city looks so empty and depressed. It seems like everyone lives in the suburbs.

See above. Even longtime residents are troubled by the empty storefronts on commercial arteries like Lorain Avenue and St. Clair Avenue. To newcomers, the vacancy can be shocking. Likewise the lack of pedestrian activity on city sidewalks – another legacy of suburbanization, the shift of retail to the suburbs and the ease of owning and driving a car here. Clevelanders' wimpiness about weather also plays a role. Streets and parks that are abuzz with people in summer seem moon-like in their emptiness in winter. Yet as you'll find on the following pages, urban living in Cleveland is coming back into vogue, and many neighborhoods are reviving.

10. It's hard to meet people. People are so unfriendly here.

Not everyone thinks Clevelanders are friendly. Some find brusqueness and reticence more the norm. They find that Clevelanders have no interest in meeting people they don't already know. This may be in part because many Clevelanders have lived in the region their whole lives, and enjoy built-in support from family and childhood friends. Many single newcomers also say Clevelanders marry and have kids younger than average, making it hard to find other singles to hang out with (p. 228). The truth about Clevelanders' friendliness probably lies somewhere in between #5 and #9 – some people are nice, some aren't.

11. The professional sports teams are really bad.

And have been for years. Decades. For a city that loves sports so much, the records of the Browns (football) and Indians (baseball) seem downright cruel. When LeBron James was in town, the Cavs (basketball) offered hope, but even they never seemed to reach their full potential.

12. Everyone's so down on their own city.

It's been a tough half-century for Cleveland. Internal hardships – a faltering economy, emptying neighborhoods – were only made worse by the beating the city took in the press in the 1970s and 1980s. Even though the mockery has quieted, we're still like a bullied kid. We've got low esteem from years of teasing. For some Clevelanders the best offense is to anticipate and mimic the expected abuse.

13. The winters. (Teeth chatter.) Brutal.

Disclosure: I love winter in Cleveland. Winter is quiet and cozy. If you get outside to sled or ski or even just walk, it can be invigorating. But for others – especially those coming from points west or south – winter is hell. There's a lot of snow – an average of 57 inches a year, which makes driving a challenge. And between November and March, it can seem like the sun comes out... well, never. For non-winter folks who can afford to travel, an escape to sunnier climes 'round about January or February can be a lifesaver. That and, again, sledding. (For more about weather, see p. 223)

The Cleveland Orchestra at Blossom Music Center

day 57/100

ORIENTATION: LAY OF THE LAND

Lake Erie may be Cleveland's most impressive geographical feature, but the Cuyahoga River truly defines the city. The river – not the lake – has been the historic center of the city's commerce and industry, and it divides the city into an East Side and a West Side that were once separate cities (p. 13). Clevelanders love to identify themselves as East Siders or West Siders. And there's a whole slew of stereotypes that go along with these identities. The box on p. 23 lists stereotypes about who lives on the respective sides of town.

Like all stereotypes, these are half-true, but there's wide variation among particular neighborhoods and individuals. Detroit Shoreway on the city's West Side, for example, has emerged as a center for performing arts, while North Collinwood on the East is an old Eastern European neighborhood turned punk rock mecca.

The city and its suburbs lie mostly in Cuyahoga County. But subdivisions are sprouting in surrounding counties as well. The southern suburbs of Cleveland now touch the northern suburbs of Akron, about 30 miles south. Sprawl has swallowed many former Western Reserve villages – such as Brecksville, Chagrin Falls, Chardon and Hudson.

Just as Cleveland is a kind of cultural hybrid of the East Coast and Midwest, it's also a geological mutt. Generally, the closer you are to the lake, the flatter the land – on both the east and west sides. These are the Lake Plains. The far west side, meanwhile, is the easternmost section of the nation's glaciated Central Plains. This is prime agricultural land, flat as an ironing board. But from the Cuyahoga Valley east, and a few miles south of the lake, the topography turns hilly. This is the westernmost part of the Appalachian Plateau, land that the glaciers smoothed but didn't completely level. The steep hill on Cedar Road leading to Cleveland Heights is among the western-most foothills of the Appalachians. (You also go up the hill heading East on Woodland Avenue in Cleveland; the top of this hill offers one of the city's most striking skyline views.)

WEST SIDE	EAST SIDE
• White ethnic, Latino	• Black, WASPy white, Jewish
• Working class	• Professional class and old money
• Midwestern flavor	• East Coast flavor
• Punk rock	• Classical music
• Kielbasi	• Bagels

Stereotypes (increasingly inaccurate) about who lives on which side of town

Cleveland is in Northeast Ohio, and for a long time bore the tagline "The Best Location in the Nation" because of its proximity to such a large proportion of the nation's population. That moniker has faded as people have moved West and South, but the city still lies within 500 miles of 42% of the U.S. population. People are sometimes surprised by how easy it is to get to the East Coast. Washington, D.C., for example, is a hair closer than Chicago. Below is a table of driving distances to other major cities within 500 miles.

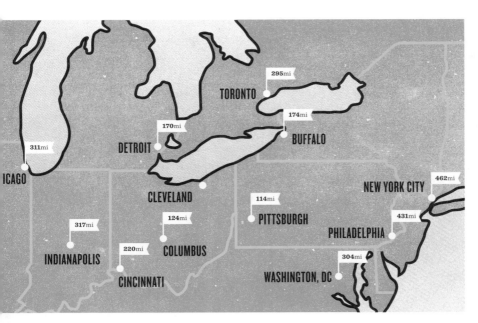

Cleveland is within 500 miles of 42% of the U.S. population

POPULATION & DEMOGRAPHICS

The population of Cleveland proper is 398,000, making it the 45th largest city in the country. This number excludes the city's many suburbs – there are 59 municipalities in Cuyahoga County alone. The metropolitan area population is either 2.1 million or 2.9 million, depending on whether you include Akron. If you do, it's the 16th largest metropolitan area in the country.

Racially, Cleveland proper is mostly a black and white city. The population in 2010 was 53% black and 37% white. Asians, Native Americans and those of multiple races make up about 10% of the total. Latinos, considered an ethnicity and not a separate race, account for about 10% of the population. Latinos are a growing presence in the city, and immigrants from Spanish-speaking countries have helped stabilize several West Side neighborhoods in particular.

Historically, blacks lived on the east side of the river and whites on the west. In the city – more than in the suburbs – those boundaries have begun to break down. Several West Side neighborhoods now have sizeable black populations.

Many Clevelanders live in poverty. In 2009, some 35% of the city's households had incomes lower than the federal poverty line. This concentration of poverty in the city has resulted from a complicated mix of social, political and economic factors over the past 50 years. For decades in Cleveland and throughout the United States, people with means either chose to live or were pushed to live in the suburbs.

But data show that Americans – especially younger ones – are reawakening to the benefits of city living. People want to know their neighbors. They want to be able to walk to the store. They want easy access to art and culture. Cleveland neighborhoods aren't reviving at the pace of those in Seattle and New York, but there are many signs of rebirth. An analysis of 2010 Census data by the Cleveland Plain Dealer showed that the city's Downtown and surrounding neighborhoods had gained population since 2000.

Luchita's Mexican Restaurant (*See pg. 190*)

day 94/100

HOUSING TYPES

Cleveland boomed between 1880 and 1920, in the era of the streetcar. Its neighborhoods are dense but nowhere near as dense as places like high-rise New York or even rowhouse-dominated Pittsburgh. Those places developed earlier, when most people had to walk to work, so housing had to be more crowded. Still, Cleveland is much denser and more walkable than places like Phoenix or Charlotte, which boomed well after the dawn of the car.

Most of Cleveland's housing is wood-frame. Masonry construction and brick siding are less common. Perhaps one reason for this is that Cleveland never had a major fire, like Chicago, so it never revised its building code to require masonry construction. Wood siding canbe charming when well kept, but residents of many Cleveland neighborhoods have chosen to cover their siding with aluminum or vinyl – understandable, given the costs of painting and maintaining wood.

The predominant housing type is the single-family, detached house. In the older parts of the city, these are mostly Colonial in style, with two stories and an attic. They have plain facades, pitched roofs and generous front porches. You can also find some Italianate and a few Federal style houses in neighborhoods like Ohio City and Tremont. The older neighborhoods also have many "worker cottages" – single-family houses built for factory workers. They are one-and-a-half stories, having a main living floor and a slope-roofed attic that often served as a bedroom. Post-war neighborhoods like Lee-Harvard, West Park and parts of Old Brooklyn have bungalows and a few ranches.

The city, along with Lakewood and Cleveland Heights, also has a large number of two-family houses, or "doubles." Up-and-down doubles are most common, typically with one two-bedroom unit on the ground floor and an identical one on the second. But side-by-side doubles exist, too. Many people prefer side-by-side to up-and-down doubles because they share a single wall instead of a floor/ceiling.

Apartment buildings generally range from four to 16 units. Contrary to what you might expect, the highest concentrations of surviving apartment buildings are on the outskirts of the city – in the Shaker Square and Edgewater neighborhoods – and in Lakewood and Cleveland Heights. Downtown also has a large number of apartments in converted warehouses and office buildings.

Less common are "terrace" houses – brick buildings of half a block or less that couldn't quite make up their minds to be full-fledged rowhouses. These are mostly rentals, but some are condos with maintenance fees.

Most housing in Cleveland dates from its boom period, between 1880 and 1930, by which time the city was mostly built out. Very little new housing went up after 1940. In the 1990s and 2000s, Neighborhood Progress Inc. – a nonprofit that oversees redevelopment efforts in Cleveland neighborhoods – decided that this outdated housing stock was a primary reason for Cleveland's continued slide in population. It helped finance scores of townhouse and single-family developments on vacant lots in neighborhoods like Detroit Shoreway, Slavic Village and Tremont. Much of this housing takes stylistic cues from the city's industrial buildings and features things like corrugated steel siding and dramatically angled roofs.

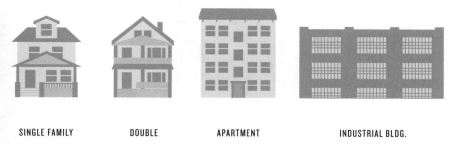

SINGLE FAMILY   DOUBLE   APARTMENT   INDUSTRIAL BLDG.

CAN I LIVE IN A COOL OLD INDUSTRIAL BUILDING?

One of the most romantic parts of Cleveland's architectural landscape is its wealth of 19th- and early 20th century industrial buildings. These hulking structures are sturdy as warships. Their floors are reinforced concrete or hardwood, and their walls are solid brick. They have enormous windows that flood interior spaces with natural light.

The factories and shops that originally occupied many of these buildings have shriveled or relocated, leaving them to sit empty or half-empty. To a new arrival from, say, New York – where people pay millions of dollars to live in industrial loft spaces – they look like a goldmine.

And, in fact, a few do now house full-time residents. This is particularly true in downtown's Warehouse District centered around West 6th Street. But these buildings have been renovated legit-style, with lots of drywall and granite counters. They may suit some people fine, but what if you want a piece of raw post-industrial heaven?

You can have it – but you may have to break the law.

It's not the city's fault. Under the leadership of Councilman Joe Cimperman in 2001, the city passed legislation to allow people to live and work in old warehouses in a "live-work zone" on the east edge of downtown. The law was supposed to be a win-win. It would allow artists and other creative folk to live in the romantic old buildings they coveted, while also fostering entrepreneurship – and potential new taxes – for the city.

But as is sometimes the case when Cleveland tries to be progressive, the State of Ohio stood in the way. The state's residential building codes are strict, and most industrial buildings can't meet them without undergoing major renovation. For artists, this presents a double problem. One, many can't afford major renovations to their living spaces. Two, drywall and new windows can wreck what made the spaces special in the first place.

In 2005, city inspectors evicted artists living in a warehouse building near Downtown because the building didn't meet state codes. Still, some artists are willing to take the risk. There are a few buildings – which shall remain anonymous – where artists keep work spaces that double as living spaces. The biggest concentration is east of I-90 in the Asiatown and St. Clair-Superior neighborhoods.

If you're just interested in renting work space, that's easy. A wealth of studio space is available in old warehouse buildings throughout the city. A small organization, ArtSpace Cleveland, even exists to put would-be tenants in touch with landlords. For more information contact ArtSpace Cleveland, www.artspacecleveland.org.

Another contact for folks interested in live-work space is Rose Management Company, www.clevelandrentalspace.com.

RENTING VS. BUYING

For people relocating from newer or more fashionable cities, the real estate market
in Cleveland can seem like a strange dream. There's lots of product available,
and at reasonable – even dirt cheap – prices. No broker fees. No zombie-like hitting
of "refresh" on apartment websites so you can be the first to call a landlord.
No waking up early on Saturday mornings and waiting in line to fill out applications
for crummy studios.

In Cleveland, if you've got an OK income and OK credit, you can live wherever you
want, whenever you want. You can take your time finding a place. When I moved
back to Cleveland from New York, I had been so traumatized by seven years of New York
real estate that I couldn't believe that a one-bedroom listing in Ohio City would last more
than a day or two.

In fact, the rental market in Cleveland has tightened significantly in the last few years.
Foreclosures have pushed a lot of people out of their houses, and they've had to rent.
As of 2011, the occupancy rate downtown was 95%, and some buildings have a wait list.
But overall, Cleveland remains a renters' and buyers' market. So relax. You have the
luxury of time.

Market highs may not be as high in Cleveland as in booming areas like the Southwest
and Florida, but the lows also aren't as low. That's because Cleveland didn't
see a glut of speculative building in the 1990s and 2000s, as did places like Florida
and Las Vegas.

If you are interested in buying, there are lots of houses for cheap. The median sale price
of a house in Cuyahoga County – which includes Cleveland and inner-ring suburbs – was
only $89,000 in 2009. (But expect to pay more than that if you want a really nice place.)

Deciding To Rent

If you're not from Cleveland – or even if you are and have been away for a long time –
my advice is to rent for at least a year. You don't have to rent an apartment; if you
want more space, there are plenty of houses for rent too. This will give you a chance
to explore neighborhoods and find the one you like best. I've heard from a lot of people

who relocated to Cleveland and either bought a house before they came, or bought one within a few weeks or months of arriving. They later regretted their decision to leap before they looked.

When I moved back, I lived in Ohio City, Asiatown and Shaker Square each for about a year before deciding where to buy. Doing that gave me enough time to let the options marinate. It also gave me a chance to establish a group of friends, which in turn pointed me to neighborhoods where they were already concentrated.

Average rents in the nicer parts of Cleveland are around $500-600 for a one-bedroom and $700-900 for a two-bedroom. The most expensive place to buy or rent is Downtown. Expect to pay a couple hundred more a month for an apartment there.

The Gospel Press building (aka Tremont Place Lofts) in Tremont day 78/100

Deciding To Buy

In Cleveland as everywhere, the choice to buy instead of rent is often as emotional as it is practical. That's probably fine. Given the vagaries of the real estate market circa now, you shouldn't be buying because you think it will be (best rational Dad voice) "a good investment." The silver lining to the thundercloud of the recent housing bust is that people aren't looking at their houses as ATM's anymore.

So what are good reasons to buy a house or condo instead of renting?

You think you will have a way of paying the mortgage every month, and you have a decent credit score (above 680 or 700).

Worried about maintaining your current source of income? Don't buy a house. Also, if your credit's not great, you'll probably get slapped with a higher interest rate.

You want more control over what you do to the property.
You're tired of asking landlords if you can paint your walls, or plant a vegetable garden. You're tired of waiting for them to repair leaky faucets and broken water heaters. You want to feel like your efforts to keep the place clean and in good general repair are benefitting you, not The Man.

You're looking for a stronger sense of community, and are ready to make a commitment to a particular neighborhood.
Homeowners are often – though not always – more committed than renters to their houses and neighborhoods. Compared with renters, they stay in one place longer and get to know their neighbors better. This can have both emotional and practical benefits. On the emotional side, you get to feel like part of a stable community – increasingly difficult to do in American society. On the practical side, neighbors may look out for your house while you're on vacation, for example, or bring you leftover vegetables from their garden.

You want a yard or a garden – and you're willing to do the hard work of maintaining it.
First, I should say that being a renter and having a yard are not mutually exclusive in Cleveland. There are many renters who have access to all or part of a yard. But if you're renting in an apartment house or high-rise, you may be starved for your own bit of green. Just be sure you're aware that maintaining a yard is hard work. There's planting, weeding, watering, raking leaves, shoveling snow – and the bigger the property, the more hours you'll devote.

Some of the denser city neighborhoods – Ohio City, Tremont, Asiatown, Little Italy – offer a compromise. Typical houses there have no front yards and only small (often paved) backyards. They may offer a place to sit outside but less green to maintain.

You plan to stay in the house for at least five years – maybe more like 10.
For one thing, if you don't stay at least five years, you're less likely to reap the benefits of being part of a community (see #3). For another, in the first 10 years or so of a 30-year

mortgage you're mostly paying interest. The principle – the amount you actually owe – stays largely the same. There are agent fees and closing costs to consider, too. Moving after only a few years makes it more likely you'll be writing a check to "sell" your house.

Your mortgage payment will be less than your rent – and in return you'll get more space/a better neighborhood/whatever. But beware of hidden costs.
Let's say you're paying $900 to live in a two-bedroom apartment Downtown. You find a house you love in Detroit Shoreway for $150,000. After you put 20% down, your monthly mortgage payment would be about $875 (assuming 6% interest and 1.25% property taxes). Hey – looks like you're saving $25 a month to live in a house you love in a neighborhood you like.

But don't forget to consider utilities and the more hidden costs of home ownership. Sure, there's gas and electricity, which you were probably already paying as a tenant. But if you're now heating and lighting a big house, your energy bills will probably go up (especially if the place isn't insulated well; Cleveland winters are cold). Are you remembering – gasp – that homeowners buy their own water (count on $20 a month)? Or that if you have a security system installed, you'll pay for monthly upkeep ($30 a month)? And then there are the seemingly endless trips to the hardware store... and the handyman... That $25 monthly savings may evaporate fast.

Cleveland, Lakewood, and Cleveland Heights also offer property tax abatement programs (pg. 82) that are worth exploring.

Our culture still considers homeownership part of The American Dream. For some people, especially those from more expensive cities where buying even a cardboard box on the sidewalk is a pipe dream, the prospect of owning a big ol' house in Cleveland can be alluring. Don't be rash. Take a deep breath. Step away from the real estate ads until you're feeling calmer.

Now, some lucky folks may be able to afford to buy a house with all cash. In Cleveland, this is perhaps more realistic than in many other cities. In these cases, the equations may change. Not having to worry about rent or a mortgage is a pretty sweet deal. But again, be sure you're considering the whole picture. If that $20,000 house you saw on Realtor.com has had its copper pipes ripped out and needs a new roof and furnace and it's in a not-great neighborhood – and at $20,000, it's most likely all of the above – again, take a deep breath and consider moving on.

NEIGHBORHOODS

Now to the fun part: Where should you live? One of the things that makes Cleveland special is that although some parts of the city are struggling, there's still a wide range of vibrant neighborhoods to pick from.

An oddity of Cleveland is that these cool parts of town are scattered around in little pockets. This is good because there are nodes of activity to explore everywhere. But it's bad because it prevents a critical mass of energy from building and gives the impression of lots of blank space. Taken as a whole, though, Cleveland has as much to offer as any big city.

There's an adage that Cleveland is a city of neighborhoods. That's still true to an extent. Many neighborhoods have distinct personalities and architectural styles. But declining density in the city proper and the advent of big box retail has meant that people often cross neighborhood boundaries to meet their daily needs. People who live in Tremont, for example, are likely to go grocery shopping in Ohio City and to see movies and plays in Detroit Shoreway or Downtown. This crossing of historical neighborhood boundaries may have negative environmental impacts (more travel = more carbon emissions). But the upside is that many Clevelanders now have a stake in multiple neighborhoods, creating opportunity for less parochialism.

In the following pages, you'll find descriptions and statistics for neighborhoods in Cleveland, Lakewood and Cleveland Heights that I believe are most attractive for people

398,000

{ population of Cleveland }

1,291/100k
Violent Crime Rate
per 100k population

5,080/100k
Property Crime Rate
per 100k population

Population and crime statistics are from 2010 and are from the website of Northeast Ohio Community and Neighborhood Data for Organizing (NEOCANDO), run by Case Western Reserve University. It's helpful to compare these statistics to figures for the City as a whole, which are as follows.

who are new (or newly returned) to Cleveland. This is not meant to be an exhaustive guide to all neighborhoods in the city. There are a lot of great neighborhoods not on this list, and you'll benefit from doing some exploring on your own.

The list starts with Downtown and moves outward from there. The closer-in neighborhoods come first, and the neighborhoods farthest from Downtown are last. (Note, though, that each neighborhood discussed here, including Lakewood and Cleveland Heights, still lies within 12 miles of Downtown.)

You'll find the same basic information for each neighborhood to help you compare choices. Most of these sections (Housing, Transportation, Health & Recreation, etc.) are self-explanatory. At the end of each neighborhood overview is a section called "The Once Over." These are guided walking tours designed to expose you to each neighborhood's chief amenities and typical housing. The tours should take you no more than about 45 minutes to an hour, depending on how fast you walk. I've also listed each neighborhood's Walk Score — a rating of how easy it is to access daily needs on foot, from the web site walkscore.com.

If you're moving to Cleveland, my recommendation is that you read the overview sections for each neighborhood; pick the three or four neighborhoods that interest you most; visit Cleveland before you move, and do "The Once Over" tours for your selected neighborhoods; rent or buy a place based on which neighborhood you liked best.

If at all possible, visit the city and visit neighborhoods before you move.

The Arcade in Downtown Cleveland

day 75/100

DOWN-TOWN

DOWNTOWN CLEVELAND

For about 100 years between the Civil War and the 1970s, Downtown Cleveland wasn't
a residential neighborhood at all. You came downtown to work or shop, then went back
home on the streetcar or (later) in your car. This meant that the place largely closed down
around 6 p.m. and didn't come back to life until the next morning.

Downtown is still shaking off this legacy. Although it now has a population of some 10,000,
it's still sleepy at night, especially in winter, when cold-averse Clevelanders stay shivering
inside their apartments and the office buildings are dark. But a slow evolution is underway.
The Downtown Cleveland Alliance, formed in 2005, patrols and cleans the sidewalks.
A new tax credit has sped the conversion of historic commercial buildings to apartments.
And Cleveland State University, at the eastern fringes of the center, has been building
new dorms like crazy, driving Downtown's residential population (and sightings of young
hipsters and international students) ever higher.

In fact, demand for rental apartments Downtown seems insatiable. Units fill as soon
as they come on line, and some buildings have waiting lists.

Even within Downtown, Cleveland's penchant for scattered nodes of activity holds true.
There are three distinct residential centers in the city's center. All three double
as entertainment districts, with lots of bars and restaurants. Be forewarned: This means
they can get noisy, especially on weekends. If you don't like noise, look for apartments
with windows facing away from the street.

9,098
{ population }

88/100
Downtown's Walk Score

LOCATION

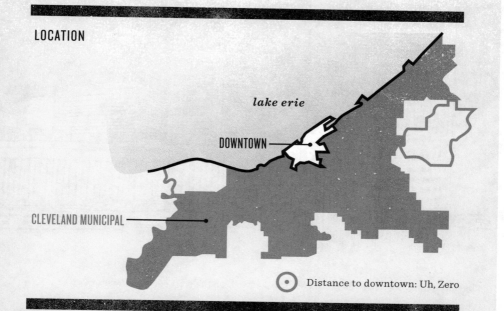

lake erie

DOWNTOWN

CLEVELAND MUNICIPAL

Distance to downtown: Uh, Zero

WHO SHOULD LIVE HERE?

Student

Professional

Empty nester

No car needed

AMENITIES AND COMMUNITY FEATURES:

Rapid Transit	Museums	Park	Specialty Shops
Grocery Stores	Retail Shopping	Yoga	Concert Hall
Restaurants	Bookstore	Bars/Nightlife	Pharmacy
Movie Theaters	Gym	Community Garden	Farmers Market
Library	Coffee Shop	Live Theater	Sports

The most populous district is the Warehouse District, on the west edge of Downtown. It has cast iron warehouse buildings that have been converted to apartments. Most conversions date from the 1990s and feature the design details of that era (think exposed brick and recessed lighting). A new-construction, high-end condo building, The Pinnacle, opened in 2005 on Lakeside Avenue and W. 9th Street. Some units are available for rent and many have panoramic views of Lake Erie. (See pinnacle701.com).

Gateway and the area around East 4th Street are near Public Square, the geographic and historic center of downtown. The district is less than a mile from the Warehouse District but feels farther because several acres of surface parking lots – a legacy of urban renewal and a thirst for easy parking – create a chasm between the two areas. Gateway/E. 4th emerged as a residential area in the early 2000s. A single developer (MRN Ltd.) bought nearly an entire block of buildings, lured places like the House of Blues to the ground floors and turned the upper floors to apartments. Other developers have since joined the party.

View of Downtown day 89/100

The third residential node in Downtown is Playhouse Square. This is the city's theater district, with five grand 1920s movie palaces that now host productions by local and touring companies. It has had a residential population since the 1970s, when developers built several high-rise towers called Reserve Square. (They were renovated in 2007.) Other buildings, including the former Statler Hotel, have since made the switch to apartments. A new condo building and townhouses have risen at The Avenue, around E. 12th and St. Clair.

A fourth neighborhood is emerging on the campus at Cleveland State, on a stretch of Euclid Avenue between E. 17th and E. 24th. At present, the area is home mostly to about 1,000 CSU students living in dorms, but there are some market-rate options as well, including University Lofts and 1900 Euclid, both around Euclid Avenue and E. 21st Street.

Cleveland's downtown architecture is beautiful in an austere, Northern kind of way. Euclid Avenue has survived almost unchanged since 1920, lined on both sides with somber

commercial buildings out of a Humphrey Bogart film noir. The civic buildings (library, public auditorium, courthouse, City Hall) of Daniel Burnham's 1903 mall plan look like little Greek temples. The Old Arcade at 401 Euclid Ave., built in 1890, has a delicate, soaring glass ceiling and gargoyled stair rails. For some, the opportunity to wander daily though this stone and brick wonderland may be reason enough to live downtown.

If you're OK paying a premium – and let's be honest, it's a modest premium compared with a lot of cities – Downtown is one of the best options for newcomers. For one thing, a lot of other newcomers live here, so you won't feel isolated. But even more important, it offers a big range of amenities and activities. The amount you can do without getting in a car and leaving the neighborhood is unparalleled in the region.

The image of Downtown is changing, but it was and is the commercial heart of the city. Banks and law offices and a few corporate headquarters have their offices here.

That sets a certain tone for the residential sector. Residents are largely professional and don't have children. Many walk to work in adjacent office towers, but a growing number reverse commute – they drive to office parks in the 'burbs, against the flow of traffic, taking advantage of downtown's easy freeway access.

Some empty nesters (older folks with grown kids) may also like Downtown because of the range of activities, the minimal need for a car, and the lack of yard work. People over 60 should also keep in mind that they can audit classes for free at Cleveland State under the university's "Project 60" program.

Housing

There are a few townhouses at the edges of Downtown – for example on W. 10th Street and in the Avenue District around E. 13th Street and Superior Avenue. But most condos and apartments are in mid-rise elevator buildings.

Because Downtown was not historically a residential neighborhood, most of these buildings are former office buildings or warehouses that have been converted to residential use. There's also at least one former hotel – the Statler Arms, in Playhouse Square.

New construction is harder to come by. A few examples include the Pinnacle Building, at 701 Lakeside Avenue, and the Avenue District's loft building, at E. 12th Street and St. Clair Avenue. East 12th Street, meanwhile, has a few high-rise apartment towers dating from the 1970s. These include Reserve Square, 1701 E. 12th St., renovated in 2008, and the Chesterfield, 1801 E. 12th St. These last two are especially popular among international students at nearby Cleveland State University.

Transportation

Downtown deserves special consideration among people who don't want to drive much or at all (p. 202). It has by far the best access to public transportation of any neighborhood in the city. All three Rapid lines meet at Tower City on Public Square, providing direct rail connections to University Circle and the airport. Most bus lines, including the Health Line, also originate in downtown, so it's possible (if often time-consuming) to get pretty much anywhere in Cuyahoga County without a car.

Bicycling infrastructure is good and getting better. There are bike lanes on Euclid Avenue out to University Circle, although they stop around E. 19th Street through to Public Square. There are bike racks outside most destinations. A bicycle station opened at High Street and E. 4th in 2011. It has showers, secure parking and lockers, though these are probably more useful to people commuting into downtown than those living there.

All of Greater Cleveland's major interstate highways come through Downtown. There are multiple entrances to I-90, I-71 and I-77, and from them you can reach I-480, I-490 and I-80 (the Ohio Turnpike). You can also access the West Shoreway (Ohio Route 2), a divided highway that takes you to the Near West Side and Lakewood, from either E. 9th St. or W. 3rd St.

Health & Recreation

Downtown has a number of conventional gyms catering to office workers and residents. Two of the most visible are practically on top of each other: Titans Gym, 619 Prospect Ave., and FitWorks, 530 Euclid Ave.

Other gyms are buried inside individual office buildings, but anyone can join. These include Rezults, inside the Terminal Tower building at 1500 W. 3rd St., and The Club at Key Center,

127 Public Square. One of the nicest workout facilities Downtown is Cleveland State University's Recreation Center, at 2420 Chester Ave. It's in a new, LEED-certified green building and has an Olympic sized pool. But the location at the eastern edge of Downtown will be inconvenient for some. There's a yoga studio, called simply The Studio Cleveland, 1395 W. 10th St.

The Cleveland Rowing Foundation has a new facility in the Flats at 1785 Merwin Ave. Most of the time, it's used by rowers from area high schools and universities, but "lay people" can also take lessons and join summer leagues. There are also plans to start kayak rentals. Paddling down the Cuyahoga River on a summer evening as the sun is setting, with the skyline as your backdrop, is an experience not to be missed.

Cleveland Plays, also in the Flats at 2316 Mulberry Ave., runs a number of co-ed and single-sex intramural sports teams throughout the city. Options include volleyball, floor hockey, flag football, soccer and basketball. These are a great way to meet new friends if you're athletic and new to town.

Green space in the city center is mostly in the form of pocket parks and the Downtown Malls – no, not that kind of mall. The Downtown malls are essentially grand civic lawns, laid out by famed urban planner Daniel Burnham in 1903. Burnham wanted them to step down all the way to Lake Erie, but at present they stop at the lakefront railroad tracks. Lovely but sleepy, the malls may get a shot in the arm through new landscaping and programming as part of the Convention Center and Medical Mart project.

Voinovich Park, around the Rock Hall and Science Center at the end of E. 9th Street, gets you to the lake but is eerily (pun intended) quiet. Perk Park, at Chester Avenue and E. 12th Street, underwent extensive renovation in 2011 and offers a shady place to stroll or eat lunch.

Eating & Drinking Out

Restaurants are plentiful, especially on E. 4th Street and in the Warehouse District. Some of the region's superstar chefs have their flagship restaurants on E. 4th Street. They include Iron Chef Michael Symon (Lola); Zach Bruell (Chinato); and Johnathan Sawyer (Greenhouse Tavern, which grows its own produce on the roof). More casual places are sparse, but Sawyer recently opened Noodlecat, 234 Euclid Ave., a Japanese-style noodle emporium, and you can also eat at the city's only all-vegan restaurant – Flaming Ice Cube, 140 Public Square. Warehouse District residents like the Water Street Grille,

1265 W. 9th St.. The coffee shops are decent, too; my favorites are Erie Island Coffee, 2057 E. 4th St., and Phoenix Coffee, 1700 E. 9th St. (closes early).

Small, interesting restaurants hide in the shopping arcades clustered on lower Euclid Avenue. The Old Arcade, 401 Euclid Ave., offers Zen Cuisine, serving fast and nutritious Asian dishes; and Greek Express, with spinach pies and some curries. Inside the Colonial Arcade, 530 Euclid Ave., you'll find Indies Indian & American Food and Vincenza's Pizza & Pasta. Vincenza's makes some of the most delicious New York-style pies in town. Most of these places serve a business clientele and have limited night and weekend hours.

The two best sushi places Downtown are micro-sized Sapporo Sushi, in a cramped storefront at 1940 E. 6th St.,; and Sushi 86, 509 Prospect Ave. Both, unfortunately, are closed on weekends, when you can head to the very good Ginza Sushi House, 1105 Carnegie Ave., or the trendy Sushi Rock, 1276 W. 6th St.

Bars cater more to visitors from the suburbs than to Downtown residents themselves. Clubs pound out house music on weekends in the Warehouse District, while some bars seem to have a 1:1 ratio of plasma TV's to patrons. Maybe the best option is Flannery's, 323 Prospect Ave. Many Downtown residents beat a path to Tremont, Ohio City, Detroit Shoreway and Coventry to get their drink on.

Arts and culture are good, though not on par with University Circle (p. 126). There's the aforementioned Playhouse Square, around E. 14th St. and Euclid Ave., which has plays and music concerts throughout the week. The Rock & Roll Hall of Fame, 1100 E. 9th St., and the neighboring Great Lakes Science Center, 601 Erieside Ave., have permanent and rotating exhibits; the Rock Hall sometimes has concerts. House of Blues, 308 Euclid Ave., hosts national music acts of the pop and blues variety, and Tower City has an 11-screen cinema, 230 W. Huron Rd., that shows mostly mainstream fare. If you're feeling higher-brow, it's easy enough to hop the Rapid or the Health Line for University Circle.

Groceries & Shopping

Shopping, as in all of Cleveland proper, fails to impress but is improving. Tower City, in the historic Terminal Tower, opened in 1990 as a glamorous, high-end mall. A Dollar (as in "Everything's A...") has now taken the place of Hugo Boss, but some stalwarts remain – for example Brooks Brothers, Jones New York, Victoria's Secret and FYE (music and games).

Spring in Cleveland day 14/100

Dredger's Union, a new, independently-owned department store, opened in 2011 at 2043 E. 4th St. It offers hip men's and women's clothing and housewear. Cleveland designer Sean Bilovecky conceives most of the store's menswear; you can also buy tailored suits here. There has been talk of luring outlet stores to occupy empty storefronts on Euclid Avenue, but little action to date. There's a home furnishing store called Surroundings Home Décor at 850 W. St. Clair Ave.

There's no Whole Foods or Trader Joe's, which some might consider a blessing, but grocery options are decent. Constantino's, 1278 W. 9th St., is a locally owned market offering nice prepared foods, lots of wine and craft beers and limited produce. A smaller store, Simply Food inside Reserve Square at 1701 E. 12th St., peddles the basics to a less yuppie clientele. In summer months, two weekly farmer's markets (p. 92 for more on local food) supplement the stores. One happens on Fridays, 11 a.m. to 2 p.m., on Public Square. The other is bigger and happens on Thursdays, 11 a.m. to 2 p.m., at Cleveland State University (Euclid Avenue and E. 21st Street).

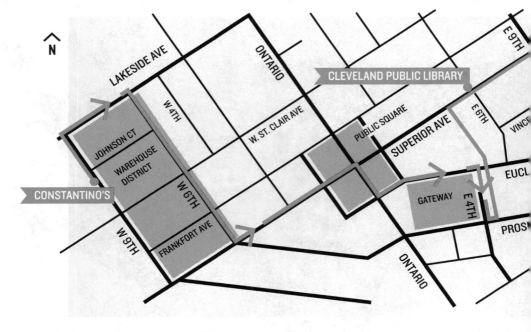

Maybe my favorite downtown amenity is free: the Cleveland Public Library, 325 Superior Ave. I first visited it in high school, to research a paper on William Blake. Even for people who don't love books, it's hard not to be taken with the magnitude and architectural grace of the second largest public library in the country. And, hey – free music, movies and books! A lovely Reading Garden – designed by Maya Lin – sits between the original and new buildings, but is only open in warm weather.

Downtown: The Once Over

The most vibrant time to visit Downtown is the weekday lunch hour, from noon to 1 p.m., when office workers venture out for food and fresh air. But to get a better feel for what it's like to live here, come at dinner or on the weekend.

Start at Constantino's Market, 1278 W. 9th St. Could you handle shopping here? The store is in the Bingham Building, one of the Warehouse District's nicer buildings. Call ahead (216-579-4000) and check out an apartment.

Round Lakeside Avenue, past the Pinnacle Building, to W. 6th St. The two blocks of West 6th between Lakeside and Superior have restaurants, some thump-thump clubs and lots of converted apartments.

Go east on Superior to Public Square. Tower City, 230 W. Huron Rd., offers some chain clothing stores, and there's a mainstream cinema – Tower City 11 – in the back. Also check out the main Rapid Station, in the middle of the mall. This would be your main public transit link to points East and West. If you like, you can visit the Terminal

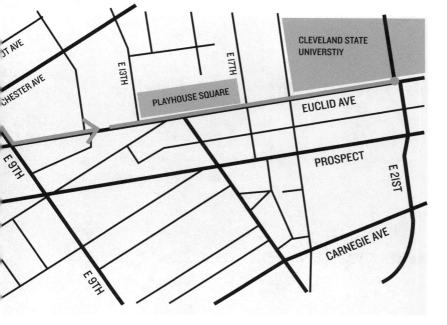

Tower Observation Deck for sweeping views of Downtown, the lake and the entire region. (You have to buy tickets for the observation deck in advance – visit www.towercitycenter.com.)

Head East from Public Square down Euclid Avenue, past the spire of the Soldiers and Sailors Monument. Wander down the short block of E. 4th Street between Euclid and Prospect. You can look at an apartment or two here by calling 216-589-1111. If you're hungry, stop at one of the street's many restaurants. If you're a sports fan, and time things right, you can check out the Cleveland Indians at Progressive Field or the Cavaliers at Quicken Loans Arena, both a block south on E. 4th.

Double back to Euclid and walk through the Old Arcade, directly across from E. 4th. Gape at the grandeur within.

Exit the Arcade on the other side, on Superior. You'll be standing across from the Cleveland Public Library. Don't miss the vaulted reading room in the original building, 325 Superior Ave. All this could be at your fingertips!

Head down Superior to E. 9th. From here you can detour to the Rock Hall and the Great Lakes Science Center, several blocks to the North (left). Walk East on Euclid, through a few blocks of mostly vacant buildings, to Playhouse Square. Visit the box office at 1501 Euclid Ave. Would the performance schedule here scratch your cultural itch? Check out an apartment in the Statler Arms by calling 216-696-6800, or the Osborn Building at 866-477-6481.

If you still have time, keep heading East down Euclid Avenue through the campus of Cleveland State University. Perhaps the nicest market-rate residential option here is University Lofts, at E. 21st St. Call The Coral Company at 216-407-8689 for an appointment.

If you don't feel like walking all the way back to Constantino's, you can hop on the E-Line Trolley, a free green bus, at E. 21st and Euclid. It will shuttle you back to your starting point. (Trolleys run Monday through Friday from 7 a.m. to 7 p.m.; on weekends you'll have to catch the Health Line, which costs $2.25 per ride, back to Public Square.)

MIDTOWN

Midtown sits roughly between Downtown and the Cleveland Clinic campus around E. 79th St. Its main street is Euclid Avenue, but the neighborhood also extends to Chester, Euclid, Prospect and Carnegie avenues.

Although it's still known mostly as a hub for business and industry, Midtown has some of the loveliest multifamily housing in Cleveland. Prospect Avenue between E. 30th and E. 55th streets, in particular, has beguiling old apartment buildings and even a few – four, to be exact – East Coast-style rowhouses. (The latter are near the intersection of Prospect and E. 36th St. Blink and you'll miss them.) Rents are cheaper than in Downtown or University Circle, with some nice 1-bedrooms available for around $500 a month, including utilities.

One of the nicer buildings is Dixson Hall, 3814 Prospect Ave., which has grand apartments dating from around 1910. One-bedrooms go for about $550, including heat. Call 216-323-7522 for a viewing.

The neighborhood's other main asset is its proximity to both Downtown and University Circle. The new Health Line bus rapid transit on Euclid Avenue will get you to either employment hub within 10 minutes, and the drive is even shorter. Euclid also has well-marked bicycle lanes for the more active.

Amenities within the neighborhood itself are scarce. Hot Sauce Williams, a beloved barbeque restaurant, is at 7815 Carnegie Ave. Otherwise, the nearest grocery stores, restaurants and bars are in Asiatown and Downtown. In fact, you'll find yourself traveling to do just about anything other than sleep. But for some, the combination of great architecture, cheap rents and quick commutes may be worth the trade-off.

Hot Sauce Williams

day 15/100

Visible Voice Bookstore

day 45/100

TREMONT

TREMONT

Tremont may be post-industrial Cleveland's greatest success story. In the past 20 years, its unprepossessing worker cottages, booming restaurant scene and unparalleled views of Downtown and the industrial valley have lured a flood of new residents.

Historically, Tremont covered all of the river bluff between Abbey Road and Quigley Avenue. But bulldozers plowed no fewer than three highways (I-71, I-90 and I-490) through the neighborhood starting in the 1960s. This isolated Tremont from the rest of the city, making it feel like a marooned small town. The Coming of the Roads also split the neighborhood into two distinct parts. North Tremont, above Auburn Street, has the marquee restaurants and shopping and the most expensive real estate. South Tremont is rougher, but seems poised for takeoff due to spillover development from the north.

At Cleveland's industrial zenith, this was an immigrant neighborhood. Residents walked to work in factories in the valley. They established a staggering number of churches, each catering to a different creed and nationality. Perhaps the most remarkable – and famous – is St. Theodosius Russian Orthodox Cathedral, 733 Starkweather Ave., with copper onion domes. One intersection, at W. 14th and Starkweather, has a church on no fewer than three of its four corners.

For a few years in the mid-19th century, Tremont was home to Cleveland University. The college's original building still stands at Jefferson Avenue and W. 7th St. It's now high-end apartments, dubbed Tremont Place Lofts, 710 Jefferson Ave., though in the

6,912

{ population }

72/100

Tremont's Walk Score

LOCATION

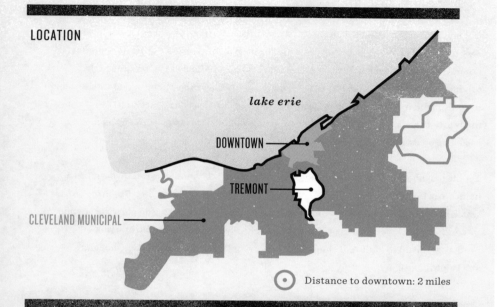

lake erie

DOWNTOWN

TREMONT

CLEVELAND MUNICIPAL

⊙ Distance to downtown: 2 miles

WHO SHOULD LIVE HERE?

 Student

 Families

 Professional

 Empty nester

 Artist

AMENITIES AND COMMUNITY FEATURES:

Rapid Transit	Museums	Park	Specialty Shops
Grocery Stores	Retail Shopping	Yoga	Concert Hall
Restaurants	Bookstore	Bars/Nightlife	Pharmacy
Movie Theaters	Gym	Community Garden	Farmers Market
Library	Coffee Shop	Live Theater	Sports

interim it was expanded and functioned as a Mennonite Bible bindery and later the home of a renegade artist. The university closed, but many of the surrounding street names – Professor, Literary, College – retain an academic flair.

The suburban exodus of the 1970s left Tremont in tatters. Dozens of houses sat vacant. Vandals stripped out building materials for resale and torched abandoned houses for sport.

Not much changed until the late 1980s. Artists began to arrive, drawn by cheap housing, sexy industrial landscapes and proximity to downtown. Theirs was a quiet immigration, unnoticed until the mid-1990s when a young chef named Michael Symon opened the original Lola (now Lolita) at Professor and Literary. Galleries and new restaurants sprang up with abandon. Here as in countless other cities, gentrification spelled M-O-V-E for many artists and poorer residents. Some renters couldn't afford to stay; many owners cashed in on escalating prices.

Yet the neighborhood hasn't gone too glossy. Even North Tremont has retained a mix of incomes thanks in part to the Valleyview public housing estate on West 7th Street, which itself has both market-rate and subsidized units. In a heartening display of economic integration, the intersection of West 7th and Starkweather has public housing units cozying up to high-end shops like Lucky's Coffee, Lilly Handmade Chocolates and Wine & Design.

Tremont is one of the most popular Cleveland neighborhoods among young professionals in their 20s and 30s. It still attracts working artists who can afford the rents (still modest by national standards) and who want to be near galleries like asterisk*, 2393 Professor St., and Atmosphere, 2418 Professor St. Some newer townhouses near the northern bluff, with views of downtown, have drawn older and more affluent residents and some empty nesters.

People with school-age kids will want to consider Tremont, in part because it's home to Tremont Montessori, 2409 W. 10th St. Tremont Montessori is a K-8 public school, run by Cleveland Metropolitan School District, so enrollment is free. For fans of the Montessori system of education, it's one of the best school options in town. Nearby Merrick House, 1050 Starkweather Ave., offers well-respected day care.

Housing

Tremont's predominant housing type is plain worker cottages, most well over 100 years old. Many of these have been split into rental units and Home Depotized – renovated on the cheap with laminate flooring and hollow-core doors. Some for-sale units have suffered the same fate, though there are more sensitive renovations to be found.

Many of the lots have both a front and a back house, typical of the oldest neighborhoods of the city. This means back yards are tiny or nonexistent – which can be a plus for the landscape-averse. There are also a few larger apartment buildings – notably Tremont Place Lofts – and terrace houses.

New construction, single-family townhouses proliferate around the northernmost part of the neighborhood to take advantage of skyline views. Many can be found along W. 5th and W. 6th streets between Literary and University roads.

Transportation

For people who work Downtown but want to live in a cozier setting, Tremont may fit the bill. It's only two miles away from Public Square, making it convenient as well for students at Cleveland State.

With its abundance of highway interchanges, it's also ideal for reverse commuters with jobs in the suburbs. I-90, I-71, I-490 and the Jennings Freeway (State Route 176) all pass through.

This isn't the greatest neighborhood for the car-free or car-light. Only one bus line, the #81, comes through North Tremont. And it's a long walk down patchy Abbey Avenue to the W. 25th Street Rapid Station in Ohio City.

Bicycling, though, is alive and well. You can easily ride from Tremont to Downtown via either a low route or a high route. The low route takes you through the Flats and the Cuyahoga River Valley, while the high route takes you across the Lorain-Carnegie Bridge. The bridge already has bike lanes, but will get much wider ones as part of an overhaul that began in 2011. Mitch Paul, one of Cleveland's most colorful characters, runs a bicycle repair shop – Shaker Cycle – at 2389 W. 5th St. Forget the Rock Hall; talking to Mitch while he fixes your bike is the most psychedelic experience in town.

Groceries and Shopping

Tremont offers a wider range of amenities than most Cleveland neighborhoods, though some – especially the many restaurants – cater more to visitors than to residents.

There's no grocery store in walking distance of the center of Tremont, though
the West Side Market and Dave's Supermarket are a mile or so away in Ohio City.
The Super Walmart, if you must, is a mile and a half south of Lincoln Park
at Steelyard Commons.

Lincoln Park is home to the Tremont Farmer's Market, one of the larger markets in
the city. It happens Tuesdays, 4 to 7 p.m., in the summer. The market fills some of the
void created by the lack of a grocery store.

My favorite store in Tremont is Visible Voice Books, 1023 Kenilworth Ave. It has
a small but impeccable selection of conventional and graphic novels, the latest nonfiction,
magazines and cookbooks – all with a vaguely punk-rock edge. The store also has a
wine bar with a small patio and hosts readings and music concerts.

For photographers, Aperture, 2541 Scranton Rd., is a fun place to explore. The store
has vintage cameras from all eras, with a specialty in Polaroids. You can also buy
instant-develop film here, even though Kodak and Polaroid don't make it anymore.

Sokolowski's University Inn day 41/100

Tremont offers at least an afternoon's diversion for women who like to buy now-ish clothes. Evie Lou, 2153 Professor St., opened in 2010. Its curator is Kim Crow, who left her job as the fashion writer for the Cleveland Plain Dealer to open the store. Powter Puff Boutique, 2671 W. 14th St., features the unique designs of its proprietor, Brooke Nieves, who came back to Cleveland from Los Angeles to open the store in 2009. Pinky's Daily Planner, 2403 Professor Ave., has the unique designs of owner Stephanie Fralick. Banyan Tree, 2242 Professor Ave., has nice home furnishings and a room of contemporary women's clothing, with a few pieces for men.

More home furnishings are for sale at Wine & Design, 751 Starkweather Ave., along with – you guessed it – wine.

Big box shopping is easily accessible at Steelyard Commons, at the south end of Tremont. This power center, on the site of a former steel mill, is a straight shot south down W. 14th Street, about 1.5 miles south of Lincoln Park. It has a Target, Super Walmart, Best Buy, Home Depot, Petco, Old Navy, GNC, Marshall's and others.

Interior of Lolita, Iron Chef Michael Symon's Tremont restaurant day 40/100

Health & Recreation

The Ohio & Erie Towpath Trail will skirt Tremont's east edge whenever it finally comes Downtown. The hike-and-bike trail follows the route of the old Ohio & Erie Canal and is one of Northeast Ohio's recreational treasures. At present it runs about 100 miles from Zoar, Ohio north through Akron and the Cuyahoga Valley National Park. Someday it will reach Downtown Cleveland via Tremont, but it's currently stalled at Cleveland's southern border. Environmental issues and Byzantine property ownership are the prime culprits.

Until the Towpath arrives, Lincoln Park and Clark Field provide green space. Lincoln Park is the heart of Tremont, a New England-style green hemmed in by houses and churches. It's always active with walkers, dogs and young parents with strollers. The city runs a public pool here, and it's a great place to walk your dog or have a picnic. The park also hosts the Arts in August festival, which presents opera, dance and classical music on an outdoor stage every weekend in August. Bring a picnic and bug spray.

Less cozy is Clark Field, a large, grassy place in the industrial valley that – true to its name – is used mostly for ball games. It's located near an active steel mill and a chemical processing plant, which provide atmospheric (some would say oppressive) backdrops. Clark Field also has a well-used dog run; it's one of the best places in Cleveland to make new friends, both canine and human. (The place is hard to find. Take W. 7th Street down into the valley, past the entrance to I-490; before you get to Quigley Road there's an unmarked access road that leads past the city dog pound back to Clark Field.)

There aren't any traditional gyms in Tremont; you'll have to travel downtown or to Ohio City for those. But there is a yoga studio, Studio 11 at 2335 W. 11th St., inside historic Lemko Hall. Vinyasa and Hatha yoga classes happen here, along with some Capoeira and Pilates.

The nearest hospital is Lutheran Hospital in Ohio City. A popular animal hospital, Gatway Animal Clinic, moved into a brand-new building at 1502 Abbey Ave. in 2011. Unfortunately, you can't make advance appointments.

Eating & Drinking Out

Living in Tremont could make you fat. The neighborhood has not only a glut of great restaurants but fantastic sweet shops as well. Lilly Handmade Chocolates, 761 Starkweather Ave., peddles artfully swirled truffles with flavors like lime and blueberry, several types of chocolate bark, and beer from around the world. A Cookie and a Cupcake, 2173 Professor Ave., is Tremont's entry in the national cupcake craze. Their concoctions tower half a foot high with frosting and cake and fruit fillings. Lucky's Café, 777 Starkweather Ave., sells delicious homemade cookies and pastries.

Coffee shops abound, and each has a distinct clientele. Civilization, on a prime corner across from Lincoln Park at 2366 W. 11th St., draws a crowd of grizzled neighborhood veterans and a few students pecking away on laptops. Lucky's Café, 777 Starkweather, has achieved national fame for its delicious weekend brunches, prepared with veggies from the adjacent garden. But at other times it has a following of do-gooders in flip-flops, sipping lattes and munching on chef Heather deHaviland's heavenly Ginger Chewy cookies. Loop, the newest entry at 2180 W. 11th St., has a record shop on its upper floor and draws young folks with choppy haircuts and big glasses.

You could spend weeks exploring the neighborhood's many fine restaurants. Some highlights include Dante, 2247 Professor Ave., with modern American cuisine; the aforementioned Lolita, 900 Literary Rd.; Parallax, 2179 W. 11th St., which specializes in seafood; Lago, 2221 Professor Ave., serving up Northern Italian dishes; Fahrenheit, 2417 Professor Ave., with modern American food; and the cozy Bistro on Lincoln Park, 2391 W. 11th St.

The bars are also some of the coolest in the city. My favorite is Prosperity Social Club, 1109 Starkweather Ave., which has an intact, circa-1940 interior and a sweet patio. Its delicious take on pub food includes vegetarian empanadas and potato pancakes. Lava Lounge, 1307 Auburn Ave., had its heyday about 10 years ago but still draws a fun crowd on weekends. Tremont Tap House, at the edge of North Tremont on 2572 Scranton Rd., has a huge selection of microbrews and nouveau pizza. The South Side, 2207 W. 11th St., is popular with a sporty, college-age crowd, while 806 Martini & War Bar, 806 Literary Rd., keeps things classy.

As for arts and culture, The Ukrainian Museum-Archives, 1202 Kenilworth Ave., open Tuesday through Saturday, has mementos from the neighborhood's time as a hub for immigrants from Eastern Europe. The Christmas Story House, 3159 W. 11th St. in South Tremont, was used in the movie *The Christmas Story*, largely filmed in Cleveland. It's popular with families and tourists; for residents it offers a place to buy fish-net stocking lamps for the holidays.

There's a small but active branch of the Cleveland Public Library at 850 Jefferson Ave.

Tremont: The Once Over

Tremont is busiest on weekend nights, when suburbanites swarm off the I-71 and I-90 exit ramps to valet their cars in front of fancy restaurants. A more representative time to come would be in the middle of the day, either during the week or a weekend, or on a weeknight.

The street grid in Tremont is funky, so it's probably a good idea to bring this book or a map with you.

Begin your walk at Visible Voice Books, 1023 Kenilworth Ave. Check out the selection here, then walk half a block west to the corner of W. 11th and Kenilworth. Across the street is Lincoln Park.

Turn right (North) on W. 11th. At the corner of W. 11th and Literary, make sure to note Lemko Hall (built 1909), which along with St. Theodosius is Tremont's most distinctive architectural landmark. It's now home to a yoga studio and condos. Walk another block north on W. 11th to Loop, 2180 W. 11th St. Grab a cup of coffee and browse the diverse collection of CDs and records upstairs.

Leaving Loop, take Fairfield a block East to the three-way intersection of Fairfield, W. 10th and Professor. Here you'll find A Cookie and a Cupcake; indulge if you like! Head down Professor Street. You'll hit Literary in a block. If you're interested in new construction townhouses, take a side trip to the left on Literary. There's a lot of new stuff on W. 7th, W. 6th and W. 5th streets.

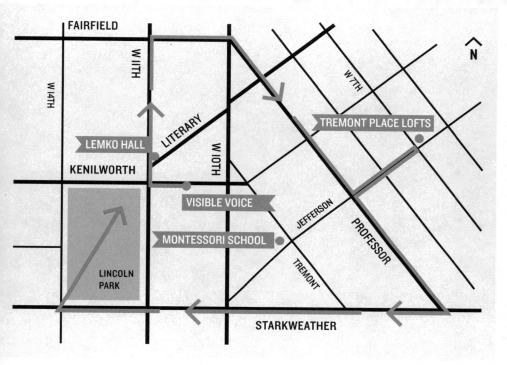

Back on Professor, keep walking southeast, your back to the skyline. You'll pass a number of churches, galleries, restaurants and shops. Turn left on Jefferson and walk for a block to W. 7th. At this intersection is Tremont Place Lofts, the former Cleveland University and Gospel Press book bindery. Call 216-274-0866 to see the apartments.

Return to Professor and keep going until it dead ends into Starkweather. At and around this intersection are Lucky's Coffee, Lilly Handmade Chocolates and Wine & Design. A block or two to your left on Starkweather are St. Theodosius Church, completed 1913 – look for the onion domes – and the Valleyview mixed income development.

Take Starkweather to the right (West). If you have kids, head right on Tremont Avenue. At the corner of Tremont and Jefferson, see the large building of Tremont Montessori. Contact the school at 216-621-2082 for more information.

Back on Starkweather, keep heading west back toward Lincoln Park. On your left you'll pass Prosperity Social Club and the former Lincoln Park Baths. These were traditional Russian baths, now converted to condos. At Starkweather and W. 14th you'll find the churchiest intersection in town, along with Bac Restaurant, Powterpuff and Jewel Heart Cleveland (a storefront Buddhist center).

Take the diagonal path through Lincoln Park to return to Kenilworth and W. 11th, where you can regroup at either Civilization or Loop.

ASIATOWN

Wonton Gourmet & BBQ

day 31/100

ASIATOWN

Asiatown is one of my favorite places in Cleveland. It exemplifies what's most exciting to me about city living: the ability for outwardly dissimilar people to live peaceably in close quarters, against a backdrop of stunning (if sometimes crumbling) architecture. This place makes a happy home for people of many ethnicities and cultures, including Asian immigrants, artists, African Americans, Eastern Europeans and Appalachians.

Don't come here expecting San Francisco's Chinatown or New York's Canal Street. Asiatown is more spread out than either of those places, and it's set up more to serve the regional Asian population than tourists. Its treasures require some searching out. Also, the Asian population here is diverse, hailing not just from China but from Korea and Vietnam – hence "Asiatown" rather than "Chinatown."

Like Tremont and Slavic Village, this section of town was built in the late 19th century for immigrants who lived in inexpensive but sturdy worker cottages and walked to work in nearby factories. In previous generations, those immigrants were mostly of Eastern European descent, and their legacy can still be seen in the area's churches and older storefronts (See St. Josaphat Polish Catholic Church at 1433 E. 33rd St. – now an art gallery – and the Croatian Tavern at E. 33st and St. Clair).

Many of Asiatown's factories are still operating. This is at least part of the reason it remains attractive to foreign-born newcomers. You can still move to Asiatown without a car or the ability to speak English and get a job with a nearby manufacturer.

4,103

{ population }

LOCATION

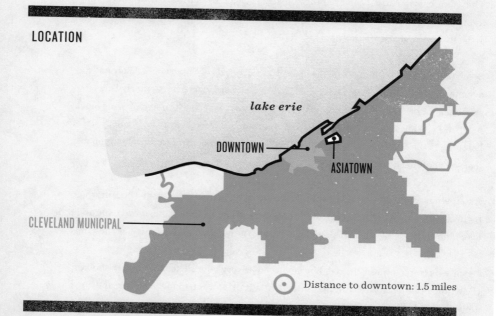

lake erie

DOWNTOWN ←

ASIATOWN

CLEVELAND MUNICIPAL —

Distance to downtown: 1.5 miles

WHO SHOULD LIVE HERE?

Student

Artist

No car needed

AMENITIES AND COMMUNITY FEATURES:

Rapid Transit	Museums	Park	Specialty Shops
Grocery Stores	Retail Shopping	Yoga	Concert Hall
Restaurants	Bookstore	Bars/Nightlife	Pharmacy
Movie Theaters	Gym	Community Garden	Farmers Market
Library	Coffee Shop	Live Theater	Sports

Not all of the old industrial buildings are occupied by traditional manufacturers, though. Artists have been trickling into this neighborhood for decades, lured by empty space in the city's largest surviving concentration of late 19th and early 20th century warehouses and factories. Some artists just work here; others both live and work. Many artists open their studios to the public at the holidays and offer their wares for sale as gifts. This is a great time to get a peek at these soaring spaces, even if you're not interested in living in one. Check the web site of City Artists at Work for more details. (For more about artist live-work space, see p. 27.)

Some fantastic old buildings line the cross-town arterials of Superior, St. Clair and Payne avenues. Tyler Village, at Superior and E. 36th (see below), is a particularly fine specimen. But the greatest bounty may be on little-visited Hamilton Avenue, one block north of St. Clair. Wandering the blocks of Hamilton between E. 30th and E. 55th streets, listening to the tapping and whirring of small-scale manufacturers and artists, you may feel you've stepped back in time.

Asiatown is about two miles East of Downtown. Its center is between the Innerbelt highway (roughly E. 24th Street) and E. 55th Street, and between Chester Avenue and the lake. The blocks between E. 30th and E. 45th are the quietest and regarded as the safest.

Despite its compactness, the neighborhood can be very quiet. There are better choices (Downtown, Ohio City, Detroit Shoreway, Little Italy, Coventry) for those looking for active nightlife or a sense of bustle.

Housing

Rental and sales options in the heart of Asiatown can be tough to find, especially if you're an English speaker. That's partly because units pass quietly from immigrant family to immigrant family, under the radar of mainstream publications like the Plain Dealer, Scene and Craig's List. You can find some postings on bulletin boards in Asia Plaza, 2999 Payne Ave., and in Koko Bakery, 3710 Payne Ave., but these are often in Korean or Chinese. Walking neighborhood streets and keeping your eyes peeled for "For Rent" signs may yield additional phone numbers.

Housing is mostly single-family worker cottages and some doubles. There are also a few legal warehouse conversions. Try LoftWorks, 1667 E. 40th St., at 216-432-0009. Payne Avenue Lofts, 3608 Payne Ave., is a for-sale condo building with beautiful wood floors and a great location across the street from Dave's Supermarket, Tink Holl and Koko Bakery (see below); contact Progressive Urban Real Estate at 216-619-9696. Tower Press, 1900 Superior Ave., is a former Wooltex factory that's technically Downtown but near Asiatown. It has a gym and coffee shop. Its units are all rentals. Call 216-241-4069 for an appointment.

Transportation

The neighborhood is among the city's most highway-accessible. You can easily reach I-90, I-71 and I-77 and the West Shoreway from ramps off Superior Avenue around E. 25th Street. Reverse commuters should take note.

It's also not a bad place for those who want to live car-free or car-light. There's no Rapid station, but there are buses on Payne, Superior and St. Clair avenues. Downtown is easy to reach on bicycle and the eastern portion of Downtown is a short walk.

Students at Cleveland State University sometimes choose to live here. From Payne Avenue and E. 30th Street, it's less than a mile from the Main Classroom building and the Recreation Center. Rents tend to be very cheap, an obvious plus for students. I lived in Asiatown for two years while I was a student at CSU, and loved it.

Groceries & Shopping

Dave's Supermarket, 3301 Payne Ave., isn't fancy, but it's large and has a good selection of produce. There's also a pharmacy inside.

More interesting are the neighborhood's many large Asian markets. The most notable of these include Asia Food Company, inside Asian Town Center, 3820 Superior Ave.; Tink Holl, 1735 E. 36th St. in an old warehouse building; Good Harvest Food Market, 3038 Payne Ave.; and Park 2 Shop, 2999 Payne Ave.

Kim's Oriental Foods, 3710 Superior Ave., specializes in Korean groceries and sundries.

Walking or driving through Asiatown, you may wonder: Where are all the stores? It's a quirk of this neighborhood that many of the most interesting retail shops hide inside tiny "malls." The two most notable mini-malls are Asia Plaza, 2999 Payne Ave., and Asian Town Center, 3820 Superior Ave. Large grocery stores (see above) and restaurants anchor both.

Asia Plaza opened in the 1990s and has a florist, a jeweler, a couple of gift shops and an immigration attorney. Asian Town Center opened in 2010 and has a similar retail mix (gifts, jewelry, herbs) and some gallery space. Its anchor market is Asia Food Company. It also has a couple of restaurants.

There are a few standalone stores, too. One of my favorites is China Merchandise Exhibit, 3620 Superior Ave. As you walk into this jam-packed emporium of kitsch, you're greeted by talking teddy bears and wall-clocks. For those familiar with New York City, China Merchandise recalls the popular Pearl River department stores.

Health & Recreation
Folks interested in Eastern or alternative medicine may want to check out Bai Wei Herbal Store, inside Asian Town Center, 3820 Superior Ave. Herbal remedies are also on offer at the stand-alone Jet Shing Tong, 3420 Superior Ave.; and at Tak Yuen Tong inside Asia Plaza.

The neighborhood's more conventional health practitioners also cater to a primarily Asian clientele, though they accept all comers. Smile Dental, helmed by Dr. Emily Chou, is at 3608 Payne Ave. Dr. Sheng Liu, MD, sees patients at Asia Plaza.

Nulife Fitness Center, inside Tyler Village at 3615 Superior Ave., has a weight room, sauna and boot-camp fitness classes. The City of Cleveland also operates the free Sterling Recreation Center, 1380 E. 32nd St.

Kirtland Park, 1140 E. 49th St., must be one of the city's odder and more intriguing public spaces. Its centerpiece is a crumbling stone amphitheater that looks for all the world like an Ancient Greek ruin. You can have a picnic here looking out toward Lake Erie, though the roar of traffic from I-90, at the park's northern border, detracts from the eerie peacefulness.

Eating & Drinking Out
Not surprisingly, most of the restaurants are Asian. Many places are worth your time and money. (See box, p. 71)

Most famous among the non-Asian outliers is Slyman's, 3106 St. Clair Ave., which has been serving up obscenely large corned beef sandwiches for decades. There's a soul food restaurant, Just Like Mom's, at 3030 Superior Ave. Old-school breakfasts are slung at the Fifth Wheel, 3306 Superior Ave. Tastebuds Café, 1400 E. 30th St., is only open for weekday lunches, and is run by one of the artists who lives and works in its host building. The cafeteria-style eatery is one of the most fun places to grab lunch in Cleveland.

Frank Sterle's Slovenian Country House, 1401 E. 55th St., on the east edge of the neighborhood, has long, cafeteria-like wooden tables and is also worth a visit, less for the food than the polka nights.

The best coffee shop – and coffee is only a bit player on the menu – is Koko Bakery, 3710 Payne Ave. Here you can sample red bean paste buns and teriyaki rice bowls. Jessica, the ebullient owner-manager, will be happy to mix your bubble tea just the way you like it. The lovely Artefino, in the Tower Press building at 1900 Superior Ave., offers a more Western caffeine fix. (Be forewarned: both places close early.)

The bars date mostly to the neighborhood's Eastern European incarnation. Most serve a clientele of workers from the nearby factories, but some are also welcoming to explorers. Until her death at 92 in 2006, Mitzi Jerman oversaw an eponymous pub at 3840 St. Clair Ave.; it still operates, with Jerman's big-hearted presence still palpable in the warm interior. The Croatian Tavern (3244 St. Clair Ave.) is another inviting hole-in-the-wall.

Asiatown: The Once Over

Asiatown makes for a fascinating neighborhood walk. On one block, you can hear the tink-tink-tink of tool-and-die casters and the roar of glass-blowing furnaces coming from open warehouse windows. On the next, you'll find quiet gardens where Chinese long beans reach like tentacles through fences.

Asiatown's busiest time is probably Saturday afternoons, when people drive into the neighborhood from as far as Pennsylvania and western New York to shop for Asian groceries and merchandise. This is a fine time to visit, though a weeknight will provide a more representative glimpse.

Start on Payne Avenue at E. 36th St., where there's plentiful parking around Dave's Supermarket. Check out Dave's to see if you'd be happy doing your day-to-day grocery shopping here.

Just across the street from Dave's, at 1735 E. 36th St., is Tink Holl, one of the largest Asian markets. It's an old warehouse building with Asian pillars at the front door. Check out the imported vegetables, teas and sweets.

Leave Tink Holl and walk east down Payne Avenue. Immediately on your right will be Payne Avenue Lofts, at 3608 Payne Ave., with for-sale live-work spaces. Keep walking east to the small strip center at Payne and E. 37th St. Here you'll find Koko Bakery. Also in the strip are Map of Thailand restaurant and Sun Hair Salon, whose outgoing owner will regale you with tales of her latest expeditions to out-of-state casinos as she snips your wig.

At E. 40th St., turn left (North). You'll pass the LoftWorks building on your right – more live-work condos – and a few other nice renovated buildings. At Superior Ave., turn left, back toward downtown. On your left will be Asian Town Center, with its food market and shops. You can access the mall via the large ramp on Superior or from the main entrance on E. 38th St.

Keep walking west on Superior toward downtown, to Korea House Restaurant and the attached Kim's, 3700 Superior Ave., which has Korean food, music and movies. Next door is China Merchandise Exhibit, well worth a visit (but typically not open until noon). Across the street is the red-brick campus of Tyler Village, a former elevator factory with graceful brick walkways above E. 36th. The gorgeous 19th century buildings now house an improbable mix of tenants including Indigo Imp Brewery, Ante Up Recording Studios (where Bone Thugs 'N' Harmony and Tori Amos have recorded) and DigiKnow, a marketing firm. If you can get inside the buildings, they're worth seeing.

Look right down E. 33rd St. between Superior and St. Clair. You'll see Josaphat Arts Hall, 1435 E. 33rd St., a former Catholic church turned art gallery. Its hours are mostly by appointment but the twin yellow-brick campaniles are worth viewing anytime.

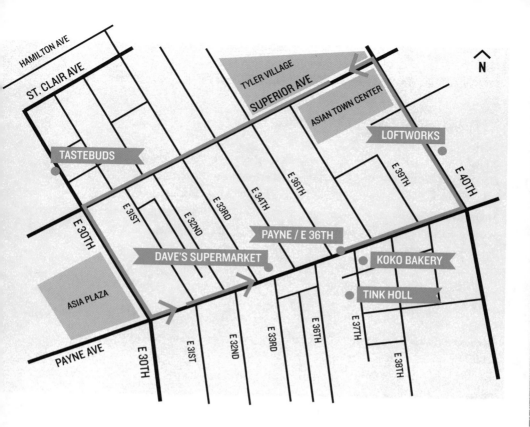

At E. 30th Street, go right (North). You'll see a large warehouse building at 1400 E. 30th St. It houses working artists and a printmaking studio, Zygote Press, which has occasional shows. If you're here on a weekday at lunch, check out Tastebuds Café, an airy cafeteria run by one of the resident artists.

Double back on E. 30th back to Payne Ave., where you'll hit Park 2 Shop and the attached Asia Plaza mall, 2999 Payne Ave. Inside the door of the mall on the E. 30th St. side, you'll find a bulletin board with apartment and house listings.

Go East on Payne for a few blocks to Dave's, your starting point.

Side trip: If you're loving the industrial architecture of the neighborhood, go north several blocks on E. 30th St. to Hamilton Avenue. Head East on Hamilton for a fascinating window into Cleveland's (and the nation's) industrial past and present. Some of the buildings between E. 30th and E. 55th still have small-scale industry; others have artists; still others are vacant. The crown jewel may be the Brown Hoist Building, at E. 45th Street and Hamilton, which dates from 1902. The massive building, distinguished by its curved front-façade windows, is still used as a warehouse.

CLEVELAND FOR THE FANCY

A lot of Cleveland is rough around the edges. Even some better-known neighborhoods, like Ohio City and Detroit Shoreway, face vacancy, crime and poverty. In most places in the city, you're likely to live near families who are struggling to make ends meet. There may be some buildings that are empty or underused. To me, these things are part of Cleveland's allure: The opportunity to live in economically diverse neighborhoods where not everyone is just like me.

But not everyone feels that way. You know who you are. You like to shop at Whole Foods. You want neighbors who have neatly groomed gardens. You're a little bit Fancy.

I have a friend who moved back to Cleveland after years in San Francisco. She bought a house in a high-end part of Cleveland Heights because she could finally afford to live "somewhere really nice." After years in a coastal city where no one but the very wealthy could afford to live in the nicest parts of town, she wanted to take advantage of Cleveland's affordability. She wanted the leafy sidewalks and an air of understated affluence.

Of course, to get Fanciness, you'll be trading a few things. Super cheap real estate, for example, and the messy vibrancy and diversity that many people find inspiring. But for some, the trade is worthwhile.

If you're Fancy, I would steer you to certain parts of town. The list below goes in order from most to least Fancy, based on factors like quality of housing, income levels and educational attainment. (Note that in Northeast Ohio, the Really Fancy tend to live in far suburbs like Pepper Pike, Gates Mills and Bay Village. As you've probably figured out by now, those places are not within the scope of this book.)

Cedar-Fairmount.
Called the "Upper East Side" of Cleveland Heights, this neighborhood has a yoga studio, a gelateria and stately architecture. It's just up the hill from University Circle, and is home to a mix of students and well-educated professionals. Fairmount Boulevard and its side streets have some of the most impressive houses in the region. Many are the former addresses of industrial barons of the early 20th century. They now shelter limousine liberals.

Edgewater.

Stately brick and stone mansions line Edgewater and Lake avenues between West Boulevard and the city border at W. 117th St. More modest 1920s-era houses can be found on Clifton Boulevard and the side streets leading to Baltic. For renters, there are nice apartment buildings, too. The retail options along Clifton are fittingly upper-middle-class – Starbucks, novelty stores, wine bars, a men's tailor.

Downtown.

Many Downtown residents are professionals – lawyers, accountants, bankers, doctors and staff at the Cleveland Clinic. The neighborhood still has its rough spots, but increasingly Downtown caters to these clientele, with an increasing number of nice shops and restaurants. The area around E. 4th St. may be the most pleasant and convenient part of Downtown at present.

University Circle.

For years, University Circle proper had few places to live. But new, high-end housing is rising like gangbusters. Redevelopment is particularly intense around the intersection of Euclid and Ford. Starchitect-designed apartment buildings and townhouses are replacing parking lots, drawing residents who want to walk to Fancy institutions like The Cleveland Museum of Art, Severance Hall (home of The Cleveland Orchestra) and the new Museum of Contemporary Art. Living here may especially make sense if you've got a job at one of the institutions or the two major hospitals nearby (University Hospitals and the Cleveland Clinic).

Coventry.

Coventry in Cleveland Heights is solidly middle-class, staunchly liberal and has the feel of an independent college town inside the city. Nice retail and restaurant options abound, of which many – like Tommy's Restaurant – have been around for decades. It's a less upper crust version of Cedar-Fairmount.

Little Italy.

Stable for decades due to a tightly controlled – some say racist – housing market, Little Italy has adorable brick streets, restaurants, shops and galleries. It's between University Circle and Cleveland Heights, and caters to the well-educated residents and students of those areas. The high concentration of students – and accompanying rental housing, much of it poorly maintained – keeps this area from reaching the higher levels of Fanciness. The nicest place to live may be the old Murray Hill Schoolhouse, now condos and rentals.

Nothern part of Detroit-Shoreway.

Detroit Shoreway as a whole remains mixed-income. But north of Detroit Avenue, between West 58th and West 74th streets, high-end townhouses have been rising faster than bamboo (which, incidentally, many use for flooring). These developments are seeking to capitalize on views of Lake Erie and the Downtown skyline. Battery Park, around Goodwalt Ave. and W. 74th Street, is the largest. The shops along Detroit Avenue between W. 58th and W. 74th are beginning to reflect this new, moneyed clientele.

Shaker Square.

Stately vintage apartment buildings like Moreland Courts, at Shaker Blvd. and Coventry, have an air of gentility. Nice restaurants abound on the Square itself.

Lakewood – West End.

A lot of young people settle in the central and western part of Lakewood, from about Belle Street west. The houses are manageable and have nice woodwork, and there are nice restaurants and good shopping along Madison and Detroit avenues. Graphic designers and rock/jazz musicians seem especially drawn to Lakewood.

Tremont.

Tremont runs the gamut from Fancy to seedy. There will always be a measure of grit here due to the smoking industrial valley on its east side. The most affluent parts of the neighborhood also tend to be the newest; W. 5th, W. 6th and W. 7th streets, near the bluff, have the most expensive housing.

West Park.

The far west side of the city proper isn't the most exciting place to live, nor the artsiest. Traditionally, it's been an outpost for employees of the City of Cleveland who wanted to live in a quasi-suburb. But it has nice brick houses dating from the 1930s through 1950s, feels very safe and is close to shopping and the Cleveland MetroParks' Rocky River Reservation.

Happy Dog (See p.102)

day 70/100

The historic West Side Market

day 23/100

OHIO CITY

OHIO CITY

Ohio City is one of Cleveland's oldest and most vibrant neighborhoods. Along with Downtown, Little Italy and Coventry, it's among the best places to live for people new to the city. Few neighborhoods in Cleveland – and perhaps the nation – offer so much visual appeal, character and convenience.

When I moved back to Cleveland from New York City, I lived for a year on Jay Avenue in Ohio City. The street's tall trees and cozy, shoulder-to-shoulder housing reminded me of Brooklyn. Just about everything I needed was within walking distance, and public transportation was plentiful.

Ohio City started as its own city – Cleveland's rival on the West Side of the Cuyahoga River (p. 13). Its first residents were German and Irish immigrants. In the early 20th century, well-to-do residents moved to larger, newer houses farther west (such as along Franklin Boulevard and in Edgewater). A more precipitous decline began with the rise of the automobile and freeways and the mass exodus to the suburbs in the 1950s and 1960s.

The neighborhood has been in some stage of revitalization since the 1970s. Progress since then has been in fits and starts, but recent years have seen the neighborhood gaining a stronger foothold. W. 25th Street, the main commercial artery, is in better shape than it's been in perhaps four decades. The street's landmark is the West Side Market, a public market that the Project for Public Spaces named in 2008 as one of the nation's Great Public Spaces. But the street is now also home to restaurants, bars, a home furnishings store, a bicycle shop and a vintage clothing store. With the Market's centennial anniversary in 2012, and new redevelopment plans for the blocks south of Lorain, the scene will only improve.

9,210

{population}

LOCATION

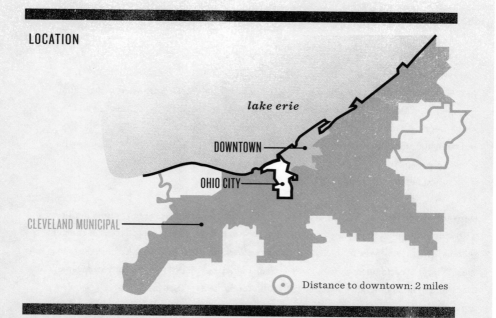

lake erie

DOWNTOWN

OHIO CITY

CLEVELAND MUNICIPAL

Distance to downtown: 2 miles

WHO SHOULD LIVE HERE?

| Student | Families | Professional | Empty nester | Artist | No car needed |

AMENITIES AND COMMUNITY FEATURES:

Rapid Transit	Museums	Park	Specialty Shops
Grocery Stores	Retail Shopping	Yoga	Concert Hall
Restaurants	Bookstore	Bars/Nightlife	Pharmacy
Movie Theaters	Gym	Community Garden	Farmers Market
Library	Coffee Shop	Live Theater	Sports

Ohio City's chief draws have been its marvelous 19th century housing – some of it antebellum – and its proximity to Downtown and the West Side Market. The chief obstacle has been a reputation for crime. Incidents are mostly of the petty, broken-car-window variety, but there have also been scattered reports of assault. This has pushed some residents and would-be residents to the suburbs. The local development group, Ohio City Inc., is addressing the issue by starting a program that will pay for neighborhood ambassadors – quasi-police officers – to patrol and clean the streets.

Want to spend less (or no) time in your car? Ohio City is among the best options in Cleveland. It has a Rapid Station at W. 24th and Lorain, just one stop from Downtown and 15 minutes to the airport. Several bus lines also connect to Downtown. A bicycle shop, Joy Machines, 1836 W. 25th St., serves pedallers. You can also walk to buy most or all of your groceries. There's the treasure trove of the West Side Market, 1979 W. 25th St., and what you can't find there will be at Dave's Supermarket, 2700 Carroll Ave. Those who want to live car-free or car-light should zero in on the area between W. 25th and W. 38th streets, and between Chatham and Franklin avenues.

Here and on the Near West Side in general, there's a growing contingent of young families with kids. A group of them recently persuaded one of the country's most respected charter schools, The Intergenerational School, to open a West Side location. Called the Near West Intergenerational School, the new school opened in Fall 2011 inside Garrett Morgan Cleveland School of Science Academy at 4016 Woodbine Ave. (See p. 231)

Ohio City is branding itself as an "Artisan Neighborhood" due to the growing number of entrepreneurs and craftsman who are setting up shop in the area. Two microbreweries (Great Lakes and Market Garden) are here, along with such specialists as Campbell's Popcorn Shop, 2084 W. 25th St., and Johnnyville Slugger, 1822 W. 25th St., a custom baseball bat maker.

TAX ABATEMENT FOR HOUSING

To help make city neighborhoods more attractive to homeowners, the City of Cleveland offers a generous property tax abatement program. This can make a big difference in your monthly mortgage payment – as much as several hundred dollars – and should be a factor you consider when deciding whether to live in the city instead of the suburbs.

For newly constructed houses, the City will waive all property taxes for 15 years provided the house meets certain green-building requirements. (You'll still pay a nominal amount for the pre-construction value of the land.) For existing houses where the renovations cost at least $2,500, you'll pay no taxes for 10 years on the improved value of the house, as determined by the Cuyahoga County Auditor's Office. For example, let's say you buy a house that the Auditor had previously valued at $90,000. You do a big rehab, and the Auditor says the house is now worth $150,000. You'll only pay taxes on the $90,000 value. For more information, visit the City's Department of Community Development at www.city.cleveland.oh.us or call 216-664-4000.

Lakewood and Cleveland Heights also offer tax abatement, though the terms are less generous. Lakewood waives property taxes for five years on new construction or renovations that cost at least $2,500 and raise the assessed value of your property. Call 216-443-7100 for details. Cleveland Heights offers a seven-year property tax abatement for certain new-construction projects.

Transportation

Ohio City has the best of both worlds: Good public transportation and easy highway access. There's the Red Line Rapid Station at W. 24th St. and Lorain, which links to Downtown (5 minutes), the airport (15 minutes) and University Circle (15 minutes). The intersection of Lorain Ave. and W. 25th St. is a busy hub for buses, too; at least four bus lines pass through, all connecting to points West as well as to Downtown.

All of this, plus the wealth of grocery options, make Ohio City one of Cleveland's best places to live without a car outside of Downtown. If you work Downtown, it's also quick and easy to bike or walk. Bicyclists flock to the new Joy Machines, 1836 W. 25th St., for repairs and general geekery; and the 100-year-old Fridrich Bicycle at 3800 Lorain Ave.

I-90 has an interchange at W. 41st and W. 44th streets. From there you can link up to I-77 as well as the Jennings Freeway – both of which lead to I-480. You can access the Shoreway (Route 2) at W. 25th and W. 28th streets.

Housing

The residential streets of Ohio City are a living encyclopedia of American architecture. You can find everything from Federal-style townhouses to Italianates to Queen Anne Victorians to contemporary condos. The exterior character of the houses is unparalleled anywhere in the city, and there are many fine interiors as well.

But be forewarned that some houses in the neighborhood's center suffered cheesy interior renovations during the first wave of gentrification in the early 1980s. Track lighting, vaulted ceilings and hollow-core doors abound. (Don't blame the renovators entirely: Many of the houses had already lost much of their original character due to abandonment and fires.)

In general, houses here are smaller than in newer neighborhoods like Detroit-Shoreway, Edgewater and North Collinwood, but about the same size as in Tremont and Asiatown. One-and-a-half story cottages –living area downstairs, large bedroom/attic upstairs – are common.

Rentals mingle with for-sale housing throughout the neighborhood. Newcomers will want to concentrate their search on the area between W. 25th and W. 41st streets, and between Chatham and Franklin avenues. This is the cutest and most walkable part of the neighborhood.

Many rentals are in split houses. But apartments are also available on the upper floors of the buildings lining W. 25th St. The West Virginia Building, 1840 W. 28th St., is a lovely yellow-brick affair and ideally located in the heart of the neighborhood; contact 216-696-3267. A small concentration of rentals also concentrate at the north end of W. 25th St., near Detroit Ave. These include the Federal Knitting Mills, 2860 Detroit Ave., and Detroit Avenue Lofts, 2820 Detroit Ave. These buildings have been tastefully renovated but can feel isolated from the neighborhood's center. Look to spend $600 for a 1-bedroom, $700 or more for a 2-bedroom.

Groceries & Shopping

No place in Cleveland has as fine a variety of grocery options as Ohio City.

Forget Whole Foods and Trader Joe's – the West Side Market is still the best place in town to experience culinary adventure. And it's got loads more authenticity and character than any chain. Meats, cheeses and prepared foods are of top quality, while much of the produce is of the "remainder" variety, but in either case the prices are unbeatable.

Pints of blueberries can be had for $2 or less in peak season – about half what you pay in a traditional supermarket. And if you go right before closing, merchants eager to turn over their inventory may sell you produce for less than wholesale. After one of these

Dim and Den Sum, one of the many roaming food trucks in Cleveland

day 63/100

late-day visits last summer, I found myself teetering down W. 25th St. with a yard-wide flat of strawberries. I froze what I couldn't eat, and ate my plunder throughout the winter.

Dave's Supermarket has a store at 2700 Carroll Ave., about two blocks from the Market. It's nothing spectacular, but has a small organic dry-goods section and a nice selection of wine and beer. Penzey's Spices, a national chain, is caddy corner to the Market, at 2012 W. 25th St.

Hansa Import Haus, 2717 Lorain Ave., offers some fun imported German dry goods and chocolate. More options have arrived to take advantage of the neighborhood's identity as a food mecca. These include Maggie's Vegan Bakery, 1830 W. 25th St.; Campbell's Popcorn Shop, 1979 W. 25th St., and the popular Mitchell's Ice Cream, set to open a shop and factory in 2012 at 2084 W. 25th St.

Non-food-oriented shopping is more limited but expanding. Room Service, 2078 W. 25th St., is the kind of store that seems to have popped up on every corner in hipster cities like Brooklyn and Portland. It has fashionable home furnishings and gifts, and a smiling and helpful proprietor in Danielle Deboe. (Deboe also stages a summer and holiday festival, Made in the 216, featuring the work of local craftspeople.) Salty Not Sweet, 2074 W. 25th St., has similar offerings, but with an emphasis on sustainable living.

Horizontal Books, 1921 W. 25th St., sells overstock books at escalating discounts based on the number of tomes you buy. Family Dollar, 1936 W. 25th St., ain't fancy, but it'll cover you when you're out of dish soap or toothpaste.

Health & Recreation

Health nuts, rejoice: Ohio City is ready to get its fitness on. In recent years, a couple of new places to exercise have opened or announced plans to do so. Fit Cleveland is a personal training studio with some group classes at 3408 Bridge Ave. Its friendly owner, Kevin Smyth, may open a larger gym on W. 25th St. in the near future. Vision Yoga & Wellness, 1861 W. 25th St. opened in 2011 and offers private and public classes.

Fairview Park (don't be confused – it's also the name of a suburb) is a rather nondescript patch of green at W. 32nd St. and Franklin Ave. It has a splash park for kids and is a good place to play fetch with the dog. In one corner of the park are the Kentucky Gardens, one of the city's oldest community gardens. For $10, you can get 400 square feet to farm for the whole summer – water and even some seedlings included. Visit www.kentuckygardens.com.

For medical care, there's Lutheran Medical Center, around W. 25th Street and Franklin Avenue, an affiliate of the Cleveland Clinic. You can see doctors and specialists here for regular checkups. An emergency room is also on site. Rosewater Dental Associates has a newly renovated storefront at 2012 Lorain Ave.

Eating & Drinking Out

You would expect the home of the West Side Market to have good restaurants – and you'd be right. The flagship restaurants here tend to be clustered on and around Market Avenue, a tiny block of storefronts between W. 25th and W. 26th streets. Here you'll find the wildly popular Great Lakes Brewing Company, 2516 Market Ave. Great Lakes is notable for its interior, including the ornate main bar where local crimebuster Elliott Ness drank, and a cozy stone basement. Flying Fig is one of the best-reviewed restaurants in the city and emphasizes locally grown food. It's at 2523 Market Ave. Around the corner, you can buy delicious soup to go at Souper Market, 2528 Lorain Ave. Crop, emphasizing local fare, operates out of a stunning former bank lobby at 2537 Lorain Ave.

The beloved Nate's Deli, 1923 W. 25th St., is so old-school it doesn't have a Web site. But it serves up some of the best Lebanese fare in town, including so-creamy-it-floats hummus. Also recommended are Phnom Penh (Vietnamese and Cambodian), 1929 W. 25th St.; Alaturka Turkish Cuisine, 1917 W. 25th St., and Orale Contemporary Mexican Cuisine, 1834 W. 25th St. Bar Cento, 1948 W. 25th St., boasts one of the coziest dining rooms in the city and serves wood-fired pizzas and other contemporary comfort food.

Le Petit Triangle Cafe

day 59/100

Several restaurants also anchor the adorable intersection of Fulton and Bridge avenues. Here you'll find Johnny Mango, 3120 Bridge Ave., serving casual takes on Mexican and Thai cuisine; Le Petit Triangle, 1881 Fulton Ave., modeled on a Parisian café; and Momocho, another contemporary Mexican place at 1835 Fulton Rd.

The neighborhood coffee shop is Koffie Kafe, at 2517 Market Ave. From the name, you might fear pink booths and hearts, but the interior is cozy and dark, perfect for an afternoon of laptopping.

Two brand-new bakeries have opened their doors: Bonbon Pastry & Cafe, 2549 Lorain Ave., featuring the creations of superstar pastry chef Courtney Bonning; and Maggie's Vegan Bakery, 1830 W. 25th St.

The range of watering holes is staggering – literally. A much-touted article in *USA Today* in March 2011 called W. 25th Street one of the best places in the world for bar-hopping, ranking alongside Dublin, Ireland and Austin, Texas. Perhaps the hippest place at the moment is ABC Tavern, 1872 W. 25th St., a former working class spot now favored by rock-and-rollers and neighborhood do-gooders. There are two brewpubs – the previously mentioned Great Lakes Brewing Co. and the brand-new Market Garden Brewery at 1947 W. 25th St. McNulty's Bier Markt, attached to Bar Cento at 1948 W. 25th, has imported beers, a nice wine selection and some creative mixed drinks. Street toughs and wannabes flock to Garage Bar, 1859 W. 25th St.

For the white collar set, classy after-work drinks can be had on the patios at Flying Fig or the Market Avenue Wine Bar, 2521 Market Ave.

Touch Supper Club, 2710 Lorain Ave., is a nightclub that draws a cool, racially integrated crowd for dinner and dancing.

Around Detroit Ave. and W. 28th Street, there's a clutch of gay bars and clubs. Union Station and Bounce Night Club, 2814 Detroit Ave., is the city's largest gay club. It draws a mixed-race crowd of lesbians and gay men, and offers drag shows (including both drag queens and drag kings) on weekends. True to their names, A Man's World (2909 Detroit Ave.) and The Tool Shed (2903 W. 29th St.) are rough-and-tumble leather bars.

Ohio City: The Once Over

The once and future cornerstone of Ohio City is the West Side Market, and any tour should start there. There's an effort to expand the Market's hours, but at present it's open until about 4 p.m. on Mondays and Wednesdays and until 6 p.m. on Fridays and Saturdays. Plan your visit accordingly.

Saturday is the busiest day to come to both the Market and the neighborhood as a whole. Parking in the Market lots can be scarce on this day, but check the side streets west of W. 25th St. The quietest time – almost eerily so – is Sunday, when the stores are closed and the sidewalks mostly empty. A nice time to come is Friday afternoon, when you'll see a cross section of visitors and residents.

After you've taken in the Market, exit onto W. 25th St. Turn right (North), toward the lake. You'll pass some restaurants and shops in these blocks, including Horizontal Books and the local office of Howard Hanna Real Estate, 1903 W. 25th St. Its storefront has for-sale and rental postings from Ohio City and around. Apartments are available on the upper floors of many of these buildings. Try the Merrell Building or the Metzner Building, both managed by Cleveland Lofts – contact 216-685-1457 or www.clv-lofts.com for a viewing.

At Jay Avenue, the retail district begins to peter out. The high rise at this intersection is Riverview Tower, a public housing estate for the elderly. Behind the tower you can see Ohio City Farm. At six acres, it's said to be one of the largest urban farms in the country. In the summer, the farm offers fresh produce for sale at an on-site stand.

Cross W. 25th St. At the intersection of Bridge and W. 25th you'll see Joy Machines Bicycle Shop and the popular Ohio City Burrito, a local version of Chipotle. Beyond these to the North is the campus of Lutheran Hospital. Head left into the residential part of the neighborhood on Bridge Avenue. You'll pass Dave's Supermarket on your left, at W. 28th and Bridge. Caddy corner to this is the West Virginia Building.

Turn right on W. 28th St. and walk a block to Jay Avenue. Turn left on Jay. This is one of the coziest blocks in the neighborhood. Where the street dead-ends into W. 30th St., turn left. You'll come back to Bridge Avenue. Turn right and walk all the way to the angled intersection with Fulton Avenue. This is another nexus of Ohio City, with the popular Johnny Mango and Le Petit Triangle restaurants, The Salon hair studio and a dry cleaner's.

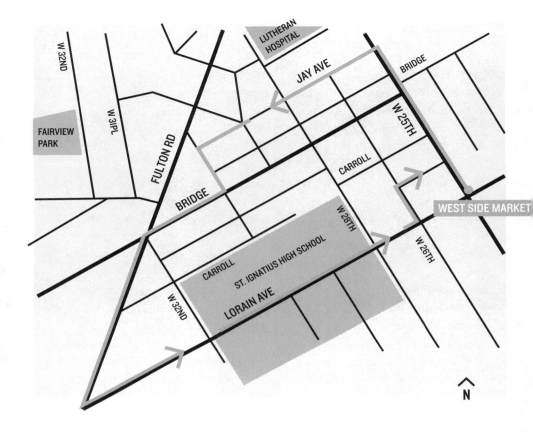

At Fulton, turn left. Pass the local branch of the Cleveland Public Library – one of the nicest in the city. It was one of the so-called Carnegie libraries, 1900 Fulton Rd. Peek in if you like. Across Bridge from the library is Fit Cleveland, a gym and personal training studio.

Keep walking on Fulton until you reach Lorain Ave. At the intersection is the ugly but useful Unique Thrift Store, 3333 Lorain Ave., which has some clothing and furniture bargains. Turn left on Lorain, toward the clock tower of the West Side Market. This stretch of Lorain is dominated by the buildings of St. Ignatius High School, a Jesuit Catholic school for boys, and a few fast food restaurants. It's not the most exciting stretch of city, but is bound to improve as development activity spills over from W. 25th St.

Turn left from Lorain onto W. 26th St., and walk a block to Market Ave. Perhaps the loveliest and most bustling corner of the neighborhood lies on Market between W. 26th and W. 25th streets. Apartments are available on the upper floors; try the Merrell Building at 1900 W. 25th St.

Depending on your taste and the time of day, stop at Great Lakes Brewing Co., Koffie Kafe, Flying Fig or the Market Avenue Wine Bar to unwind and reflect on your Ohio City adventure.

WHAT'S WITH ALL THE VACANT LAND?

In my first few years back in Cleveland, I was struck by the abundance of vacant land in some city neighborhoods. You may notice this yourself – particularly in the areas between Downtown and University Circle.

The vacancy didn't happen overnight. Developers and planners from the 1950s to the 1970s took an almost a gleeful view of demolition. They leveled neighborhoods to build highways and end "blight" (often a byword for density and minority predominance). This "tear it down" approach worsened social and economic conditions that were already driving people from the city, and sped the decline in population. Today, we're still tearing stuff down – not because of overcrowding but because of the opposite problem of vacancy and abandonment. Many houses and buildings have no one with the money or desire to maintain them.

In 2010, Cleveland had some 20,000 vacant lots on 3,300 acres, meaning 7 percent of the city is now vacant land. This corresponds with the city's decline in population from 900,000 in 1950 to just under 400,000 in 2010. For many Clevelanders, weedy lots have been a source of shame. They're scars of the city's shrinkage, a visual reminder of what has been lost.

Until recently, Cleveland lived in a state of denial about vacancy. Neighborhood plans showed new townhouses and retail districts rising on tracts of nothingness. But then came the foreclosure crisis. In 2010 Cleveland had thousands of houses on the demolition list. The magnitude of the problem – and the likelihood that it would probably get worse before it got better – finally hit home.

With government and philanthropic support, a coalition of civic groups has been reframing the conversation about vacancy. The Reimagining Cleveland Initiative asserts that the city should no longer hope for a new house to fill every vacant lot. Instead, it should promote unconventional uses of some vacant land. The city should allow urban farms, for example, to provide jobs for local people and reduce our reliance on foreign-grown crops. It should create new parks and trails, uncover culverted streams and build gardens that manage stormwater. (For more about local food, see below.)

I was on a tour recently with Marie Kittredge, executive director of Slavic Village Development Corporation. Because of the huge number of foreclosures in the neighborhood since 2005 – most of them resulting from fraudulent mortgages – Slavic Village has seen a tsunami of demolition and new vacancy. There is a silver lining to this cloud, however. Many houses in Slavic Village, as in other Cleveland neighborhoods, were built fast and cheap to shelter the influx of factory workers in the early 1900s. They remained standing well past their expiration date. Now the worst are coming down, and Kittredge and her constituents in Slavic Village can imagine a greener, better planned neighborhood.

In the meantime, here's what I realized about vacant land: It doesn't need to keep me from enjoying the parts of the city that remain vibrant. As I hope this book shows, Cleveland still has many places where people can enjoy a complete, satisfying and affordable urban experience.

EATING LOCAL

Cleveland has one of the most robust local food movements of any city in the nation. This is thanks to a cadre of passionate advocates; the close proximity of the city to high-quality farmland; and interest from the philanthropic community, which sees the potential of local agriculture and food distribution to rebuild the region's economy. In 2008, SustainLane ranked Cleveland as having the second strongest local food scene in the nation.

The tenets of the movement are that local food is healthier, more economical and more environmentally friendly. When people buy their food locally, they're supporting regional farmers. They're creating less demand for produce that's been shipped thousands of miles, from places like Chile, which in turn reduces the carbon impact of importing food.

The most visible and easiest ways to tap into the Cleveland local food zeitgeist are the countless farmers markets. Almost every neighborhood has a weekly market; Downtown has two. You can find information about these in the respective neighborhood sections of this book. The largest and most popular is the one at Shaker Square, on Saturdays from 8 a.m. to noon (see p. 162). The Shaker Square market is also special in that it has a scaled-back, indoor version in the winter where you can buy potatoes, winter squashes and dry goods. Most other markets are active only between June and October.

Community supported agriculture (CSA) programs are also becoming more numerous and more popular. These allow you to "subscribe" to a farmer or group of farmers who will then deliver food to pickup locations once a week. Geauga Family Farms (www.geaugafamilyfarms.org) is a collaborative of Amish farmers in nearby Geauga County; all of their produce is certified organic. City Fresh (www.cityfresh.org) has several pickup locations in the city and inner-ring suburbs. Heart of the City (www.urbangrowthfarms.com/csa) may be Cleveland's first CSA to feature produce grown entirely within city limits. Meat, dairy and egg CSA's are also available. The best way to find out about these is to visit the Local Food Cleveland Website at www.localfoodcleveland.org.

Cleveland City Hall has also been supporting residents who want to grow food in their backyards. Vegetable gardening, of course, has always been legal, but in 2008, the city passed legislation allowing residents to raise chickens and bees on their property. Other cities across the country have since used that legislation as a model.

If you're in an apartment and don't have space for a garden, try one of the city's many community gardens. One of the positive outcomes of Cleveland's abundance of vacant land is that there are now gardens in almost every neighborhood. Plots can generally be had for a pittance, with many providing free seedlings and water, and community gardening is a great way to meet neighbors. The Kentucky Garden in Ohio City, at the intersection of Franklin Boulevard and W. 38th St., is one of the oldest and largest (www.kentuckygardens.com). To find others, check localfoodcleveland.org.

If you're interested in making some money from farming, you can take classes offered by Ohio State University's extension program (www.cuyahoga.osu.edu). The classes will teach you how to grow and sell food. The City's economic development program also offers a program called Gardening for Greenbacks, which gives urban farmers grants of $3,000 to buy supplies and set up their businesses.

It's become almost de rigeur for Cleveland restaurants to offer dishes emphasizing local food, particularly during the harvest season. Among the restaurants most committed to the cause are The Greenhouse Tavern, Downtown; Flying Fig, Ohio City; Lucky's Café, Tremont; Fire Food and Drink, Shaker Square; and The Root Café, Lakewood.

DETROIT SHOREWAY

Sweet Moses old fashioned soda fountain

day 84/100

DETROIT-SHOREWAY

On the surface, it may appear that Detroit Shoreway has experienced a complete turnaround in the space of just a few years. Its main intersection, at W. 65th St. and Detroit Ave., buzzes with hip shops, restaurants and bars. The Capitol Theatre, a three-screen digital theater that shows art house films and 3D popular fare, opened in 2009. A redo of the Detroit Avenue streetscape widened the sidewalks, buried utility poles and added new benches and public art. Less than three years ago, almost none of this was here.

But what seemed to happen over night actually took years – decades – of planning and work. The neighborhood's renaissance dates to 1986, when James Levin opened Cleveland Public Theatre at W. 61st St. and Detroit in an old vaudeville theater. By then, many of the neighborhood's original residents – Italians, Romanians, Irish and German – had moved to the suburbs, leaving an air of abandonment in their wake. The neighborhood had become so lawless, in fact, that City Council passed a law that bars were banned along one side of Detroit Avenue.

For years, the theater operated as an isolated bright spot in an otherwise bleak urban setting. (Perhaps partly as a result, it developed a number of social programs to engage neighborhood residents, including ones that involve homeless men and youth in theater productions.)

In about 2000, Levin and other neighborhood leaders hatched a vision of turning the neighborhood into hub for the performing arts. They envisioned renovating the old Capitol movie theater, crumbling since the 1980s, into an art house cinema – a West Side answer to

14,325
{ population }

75/100
Detroit-Shoreway's
Walk Score

LOCATION

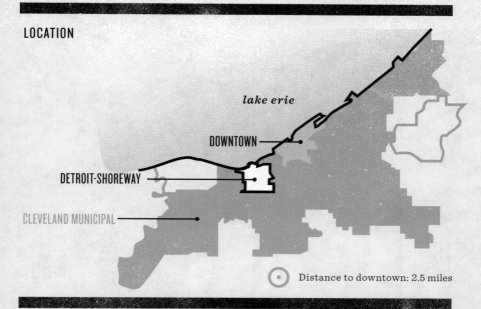

lake erie

DOWNTOWN

DETROIT-SHOREWAY

CLEVELAND MUNICIPAL

⊙ Distance to downtown: 2.5 miles

WHO SHOULD LIVE HERE?

| Student | Families | Professional | Artist | No car needed |

AMENITIES AND COMMUNITY FEATURES:

Rapid Transit	Museums	Park	Specialty Shops
Grocery Stores	Retail Shopping	Yoga	Concert Hall
Restaurants	Bookstore	Bars/Nightlife	Pharmacy
Movie Theaters	Gym	Community Garden	Farmers Market
Library	Coffee Shop	Live Theater	Sports

Capitol Theatre

day 33/100

the Cedar-Lee Theatre in Cleveland Heights. And they wanted to build a new home for Near West Theatre, a community youth theater that had been staging productions in St. Patrick's social hall in Ohio City.

Nine years later, after fits and starts, the vision is about two-thirds complete. The Capitol has opened, and Cleveland Public Theatre has been expanding and upgrading its facilities. It now owns the former St. Mary's Romanian Orthodox Church, which was built in 1902 and is the oldest Romanian Orthodox church in the United States. CPT uses the church and adjacent social hall for special events and rehearsals. Only the new Near West Theatre remains to be built, though designs are complete.

These investments – along with the streetscape project – have helped lead to the kind of rebirth that must have seemed a nearly impossible dream in the 1980s.

The neighborhood has also been working to create an EcoVillage around W. 58th St. and Lorain Ave. The idea is to build housing and amenities that encourage a socially and environmentally conscious lifestyle. So far, the most visible improvement has been a row of energy efficient townhouses, built in 2003, adjacent to the W. 65th St. Rapid Station. The Regional Transit Authority also rebuilt the Rapid Station itself to draw more riders, and there are several community gardens nearby.

The poor economy, and the focus on Detroit Avenue, has slowed additional development in EcoVillage. But the campus of Zone Recreation Center, across from the Rapid, is undergoing a $3 million facelift. Its grounds will be a kind of learning center for sustainable living.

Beyond physical redevelopment, though, two other factors have been perhaps even more important in Detroit Shoreway's renaissance. First, the neighborhood continues to be home to some of the most committed residents in the city, and it's one of the region's most racially and economically integrated.

Second, it has perhaps the best lakefront access in Cleveland – no small distinction in a city where industry and transportation separated neighborhoods from the water. A pedestrian and bicycle path at W. 65th St. leads to Edgewater Park, which has a beach and leafy picnic groves. Another path to the park at W. 76th St. should be completed by 2012. New townhouse developments have been springing up since the 1990s to take advantage of these lakefront connections and the easy commute to Downtown.

Transportation

Detroit Shoreway isn't a bad choice if you're car-free or car-light, but you won't have as easy a time as in Downtown or Ohio City.

The Rapid stops at W. 65th Street, linking you to Downtown, University Circle and the airport (the actual entrance is closer to W. 58th St., either from Lorain or Madison avenues). The station is a bit of a hike (0.6 miles) from the neighborhood's current center of gravity at Detroit and W. 65th St., and – although improving – the area around it can feel sketchy at night.

There are buses along Lorain (#22), Detroit (#26) and W. 65th St. (#45), all connecting to Downtown.

Bicyclists from the entire West Side and Lakewood use Detroit Avenue to reach downtown, and you'll see a growing number of helmeted commuters during rush hour. Franklin Boulevard is also nice for biking, and has painted "sharrows" to let motorists know to share the road. Blazing Saddles Bike Shop, 7427 Detroit Ave., does repairs.

Highway access is just OK. The Shoreway is the easiest highway to reach, either at Lake Avenue or W. 49th St., providing quick connections to Downtown and I-90 East. But to reach points South or West, you'll have to drive to the W. 85th Street entrance to I-90 West, or the W. 41st-W. 44th entrance to I-90 East (about 7 minutes away), which takes you to I-77 and the Jennings Freeway.

Housing

Detroit Shoreway prides itself on racial and economic integration, with strong populations of whites, blacks and Latinos of all income levels. Much of this is thanks to the diversity of housing stock. Well-to-do residents gravitate to the new townhouses along the lake and the grand Victorians on Franklin Boulevard and West Clinton Avenue. But low-income families also have a lot of choices. Many of the apartments around W. 65th St. and Detroit Ave., for example, are designated for low-income residents. And the side streets both north and south of Detroit have very affordable housing available for rent and sale.

In general, the best-maintained housing is from Bridge Avenue north, between W. 54th and W. 74th streets. South of Bridge, deterioration and abandonment increase – with notable exceptions like EcoVillage.

Much of the historic housing dates from between 1890 and 1920. Houses and backyards here are bigger than in Ohio City and Tremont, and prices are cheaper, so your dollar tends to buy more space compared with those places. (But keep in mind that more space equals more maintenance, particularly when dealing with historic houses.) You can buy a large Victorian in Detroit Shoreway for under $150,000 even on the best blocks – though it will likely need some love – and even less the farther off the beaten path you go.

Singles and doubles predominate, though there are some nice terrace houses (like Windsor Terrace at W. 81st St. and Detroit Ave.). If you're in the market for a double, check the blocks between W. 59th and W. 73rd St., north of Detroit. Meanwhile, Detroit Ave. itself has conveniently located apartment buildings, some specially designated for low-income individuals and families. The former Lou's Furniture warehouse building, at 6710 Detroit Ave., has income-restricted live-work spaces for artists; contact Detroit-Shoreway Community Development Organization (216-961-4242) for information.

There's a lot of infill townhouse development close to the lake, most dating from after 1998. Battery Park, around W. 74th St. and Herman Ave., is the largest and newest example. Other places to look are along W. 67th and W. 69th streets, north of Detroit, and at W. 49th and Tillman Ave. These newer houses sell for between $175,000 and $350,000.

Groceries & Shopping

As in other city neighborhoods, grocery options leave much to be desired. Save a Lot, 5901 Detroit Ave., will do in a pinch, but for major grocery trips you'll be heading to the West Side Market and Dave's in Ohio City, or to the gargantuan Giant Eagle several miles away at 3050 W. 117th St. If you're into meat, Stockyard Meats, 6105 Detroit Ave., is friendly and locally owned.

The small but useful Gordon Square Farmers' Market happens in the parking lot of Bethany Presbyterian Church, 6415 West Clinton Ave. between June and October. Hours are 10 a.m. to 2 p.m. on Saturdays. Residents have also started a cooperative egg farm and a fruit orchard, if you'd like to harvest your own eggs and berries. Ask around at the Farmers' Market for information on both of these.

Higher-end retail shops concentrate around Detroit Ave. and W. 65th St., and new stores seem to open every month. Turnstyle, 6505 Detroit Ave., has contemporary women's clothing. Duo Home, 6507 Detroit Ave., has stylish furniture and lamps. The neighborhood florist and gift shop is Petals x Threads, 6515 Detroit Ave.

Don't even think of furnishing your place without visiting the antique stores along tattered Lorain Avenue between W. 65th and W. 85th streets. One of my favorite stores in all of Cleveland is Reincarnation Vintage Design, 7810 Lorain Ave., (open weekends only). Ron and Cynthia Nicolson, the friendly owners, sell fantastic vintage furniture and architectural salvage, some of it refurbished and reimagined by Ron, in their beautiful store. Bijou Antique Gallery, 7806 Lorain Ave., in an old movie theater, sells more conventional antiques from a number of different dealers. Sweet Lorain, 7105 Lorain Ave., in an old bowling alley, has kitschy collectibles, vintage furniture and clothing.

Health & Recreation

The city-operated Michael Zone Recreation Center, 6301 Lorain Ave., is free and popular with neighborhood residents; its outdoor basketball courts are especially popular. The grounds are undergoing a $3 million renovation as of this writing. Somewhat far from the heart of the neighborhood, the Cudell Recreation Center, 1910 West Blvd., has a swimming pool and gym.

Open Yoga Gallery, 4736 Lorain Ave., offers a variety of yoga classes and displays by local artists in a serene and tasteful space. Owner April Arotin, recently returned from San Francisco, also stages outdoor classes around town in the summer. There's No Place Like Om, 5409 Detroit Ave., bills itself as Cleveland's only place for nude yoga (men only), but you don't have to take your clothes off to have a good time; traditional Hatha classes happen here as well.

Battery Park, the new infill development around W. 74th Street and Herman Avenue, has outdoor volleyball courts; contact Cleveland Plays for more information, www.clevelandplays.com.

The closest traditional gyms are downtown and in the Edgewater neighborhood (see respective sections).

Lutheran Hospital has an outpost at 6412 Franklin Blvd., offering English- and Spanish-speaking doctors.

Eating & Drinking Out

Detroit Shoreway has enough restaurants and bars to keep you well-fed and knackered for a week. For pure atmosphere and casual hipness, you can't beat the Happy Dog, 5801 Detroit Ave. The place has an interior that's gone virtually unchanged since World War II. Good live music happens here almost every night, and ranges from classical chamber concerts by junior members of the Cleveland Orchestra (called "Classical Revolution" on the schedule) to indie pop. The friendly crowd is of the cute-T-shirt-and-glasses variety. For dinner, you can eat traditional or vegan hot dogs with your choice of more than 100 toppings.

For an interior just as untouched, visit Parkview Nite Club, 1261 W. 58th St. This place brings in a mix of factory workers, motorbikers, suburbanites and folks from the fancy townhouses nearby, all drawn to the atmospheric wood-paneled walls. Live music happens on the weekends and tends toward blues-rock.

For a more contemporary, upscale night, try Luxe, 6605 Detroit Ave.; Stone Mad, 1306 W. 65th St.; and the Wine Bar at Battery Park, 7524 Fr. Frascati Dr. All three serve food and drink. Luxe is notable for its well-dressed clientele, hip in an HBO-series kind of way, and its great patio. The Wine Bar is in an airy post-industrial space. Stone Mad is a $3 million renovation of a former hole-in-the-wall. The patio – made of salvaged sandstone and with an outdoor pizza oven – is worth a visit.

Cheap, good ethnic food is available at Minh Anh (Vietnamese; 5428 Detroit Ave.), Indian Delight (5507 Detroit Ave.), and Frank's Falafel (Middle Eastern, 1823 W. 65th St.).

For dessert, everyone throngs into Sweet Moses Soda Fountain & Treat Shop, 6800 Detroit Ave. This place opened in Spring 2011, but thanks to nostalgic-without-being-cheesy interior, feels like it's been here forever. It's modeled on a vintage soda fountain, and offers homemade chocolate and ice cream. If you come with four or more friends, get the Terminal Tower – a trough of 10 scoops, oozing with homemade caramel, hot fudge and marshmallow fluff.

Gypsy Beans & Baking Co., 6425 Detroit Ave., is the unofficial center of the neighborhood. It has a creative menu of espresso drinks and some fine lunch options, but the stars are the homemade scones and muffins. It seems the whole neighborhood stops in for a snack and a pick-me-up on weekend mornings in the winter. The place also serves as a kind of "truck stop for bicyclists," serving the many two-wheeled commuters who travel Detroit Avenue on their way to or from Downtown.

Detroit-Shoreway: The Once Over

The area is fairly active all the time, but it's most neighborhoody on weeknights, when folks are home from work. Ground zero is Detroit Ave. and W. 65th St., but to avoid doubling back, start just east of here, at W. 58th and Detroit Ave. There's plenty of free on- and off-street parking.

At the corner of W. 58th St. are the Happy Dog and Latitude 41 (comfort food). If you look down Detroit toward Downtown, you can see Indian Delight and Minh Anh, as well as There's No Place Like Om yoga studio.

Walk west on Detroit Avenue, away from Downtown. You'll pass Stockyard Meats and Save a Lot. On your left will be Cleveland Public Theatre; you can pick up a schedule inside the box office. Note St. Mary's Church, now part of the theater campus. It faces West and East in adherence with Orthodox tradition.

At Detroit's intersection with W. 65th St., you'll see the Capitol Theatre. If you're a movie buff, go inside and ask to peek into the nicely restored main theater. The front desk clerk will usually let you, even if there's a movie playing.

Keep walking West on Detroit. You'll pass several shops; Turnstyle and Duo Home are worth checking out if they're open. The Lesbian & Gay Center of Cleveland, 6600 Detroit Ave., is also on this block; it offers a variety of community services and events. Sweet Moses will be on your right; stop in for chocolate or ice cream if you like.

At W. 69th St., turn right (downhill) toward the lake. You'll see some representative middle-class housing in the first few blocks. As you go farther down the hill, you'll pass through a tiny enclave of close-knit storefronts and buildings. This was and is the heart of Detroit Shoreway's Italian neighborhood.

At Father Caruso Drive, turn left. You'll see the Battery Park development ahead, marked by a restored brick powerhouse building with a tall smokestack. Here, if you're interested, you can see some new townhouses and condos; call 216-939-9926 or visit for an appointment.

Double back down Father Caruso and walk East, back toward Downtown. At W. 65th St., you'll see a pedestrian and bicycle pathway with mosaic art on its retaining walls. If you have time, take the path down to the lake and 60-acre Edgewater State Park. Here you'll

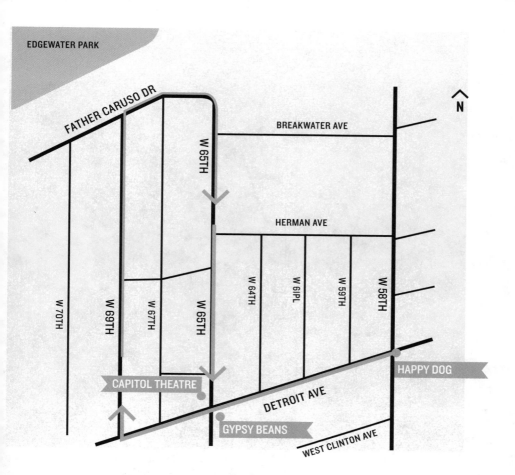

find a marina, beach and – on the bluff at the West end of the park – some nice picnic areas with stunning skyline views. You could plan to have a picnic lunch here.

Retrace your steps up the pedestrian walkway to W. 65th Street. Stay on W. 65th, going North (uphill) toward Detroit. You'll pass Stone Mad, with its stone patio, at the intersection with Herman Ave. At Detroit, you'll be back at ground zero. Take a break at Gypsy Beans.

If you'd like to check out some of the nicer Victorian houses in the neighborhood, walk a block south on W. 65th St. to either West Clinton Avenue or Franklin Boulevard. The blocks between W. 58th and W. 74th have dozens of century houses in various states of renovation. You'll also pass the Lutheran Hospital office and Rite Aid.

Find your way back to Detroit and W. 58th St., where you started.

Fall in Cleveland

day 99/100

~ old ~
BROOKLYN

OLD BROOKLYN

Old Brooklyn, a few miles southwest of Downtown and developed right before and immediately after World War II, never experienced the decline and reinvention of some of the city's older neighborhoods.

The upside to this relative stability is that Old Brooklyn has never had to deal with widespread vacancy or abandonment. It has remained a solid, middle-class neighborhood of modest houses and small parks, with touches of ethnic heritage – a mom-and-pop sausage shop, atmospheric pubs. It has little of the kinetic energy and sense of rebirth of, say, Ohio City or Detroit Shoreway, but many people will find that sense of foundation appealing.

The neighborhood still looks and feels a bit like a separate city. This is partly because the Big Creek Valley, which forms its northern boundary, divides it from the rest of Cleveland; and partly because it grew up as the independent village of Brighton. Brighton later changed its name to South Brooklyn, and in 1905 joined the City of Cleveland. Drew Carey, the neighborhood's most famous son, still owns a house here. (Just north of Old Brooklyn lies the older neighborhood of Brooklyn Centre – see box, p. 115)

Old Brooklyn's historic commercial heart is the intersection of Pearl and Broadview roads. (Pearl Road is the name for W. 25th Street south of I-71.) This intersection was originally Brighton's downtown, and is one of Cleveland's coziest "urban rooms," hemmed in by solid old brick buildings and churches. Many of the storefronts are dark at present.

32,009
{ population }

LOCATION

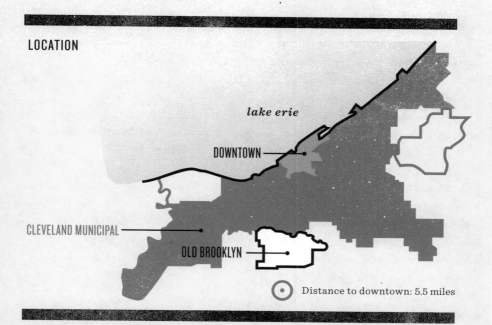

lake erie

DOWNTOWN

CLEVELAND MUNICIPAL

OLD BROOKLYN

Distance to downtown: 5.5 miles

WHO SHOULD LIVE HERE?

Families

Professional

Empty nester

AMENITIES AND COMMUNITY FEATURES:

Rapid Transit	Museums	Park	Specialty Shops
Grocery Stores	Retail Shopping	Yoga	Concert Hall
Restaurants	Bookstore	Bars/Nightlife	Pharmacy
Movie Theaters	Gym	Community Garden	Farmers Market
Library	Coffee Shop	Live Theater	Sports

The neighborhood has some well-regarded public schools, including Ben Franklin Elementary School, 1905 Spring Rd., and William Cullen Bryant Elementary School, 3121 Oak Park Ave. Parents also speak highly of the Old Brooklyn Community School, consistently rated "Excellent" in annual rankings, a charter elementary and middle school at 4430 State Rd. (For more about schools see p. 231.)

Little-known perk: If you live in Old Brooklyn, you'll get free wi-fi Internet access under a new program called "Old Brooklyn Connected." The City of Cleveland funds the program, and is considering rolling it out to other neighborhoods in coming years.

Transportation

Three different highways ring Old Brooklyn, making it one of the most convenient places in the city for car commuting. And because the neighborhood lies almost directly south of Downtown, you're close to destinations on both the East and West sides.

I-71, on the neighborhood's north side, runs between Downtown and the airport before continuing on to Columbus. I-480, on the southern boundary, is Cleveland's "outerbelt" highway and provides access to the East and West side 'burbs. And the Jennings Freeway, Route 176, on Old Brooklyn's east boundary, runs directly south from Tremont to the suburb of Parma. (It's also easy to reach I-90 either via I-71 or from a separate entrance further north on W. 25th Street.)

Public transit is adequate. There are no Rapid stations nearby, but RTA runs buses on several neighborhood arterials (e.g. Pearl Road, Broadview Road, State Road and Ridge Road) that will get you Downtown in about 20 minutes.

Pearl Road/W. 25th Street provides a decent bicycle commute to Downtown, five or six miles away. Limited recreational biking and hiking trails are available in Brookside Reservation and the Cleveland MetroParks Zoo.

Housing

The oldest sections of the neighborhood are east of Fulton Road, with houses dating from the 1920s and earlier. Single family houses in the vernacular Cleveland Colonial style predominate here, though doubles pop up too.

The two most upscale sections – though both are very affordable by national standards – nestle in the far northwest and southeast corners of the neighborhood. Brookside, in the northwest, is at the southern edge of Brookside Reservation, north of Memphis Avenue. Tidy brick bungalows and Colonial houses, most dating from the 1920s and 1930s, line Brookside Avenue and the side streets to the West.

South Hills, in the southeast, has similar stock on a slightly grander scale. Some of the houses here wouldn't look out of place in the tony East Side suburb of Shaker Heights. The curvilinear South Hills Drive forms the section's backbone.

West of Fulton and south of Memphis Avenue, you'll find modest post-war bungalows. These are well-kept and quite affordable.

There are noticeably fewer pre-war apartment buildings than in other parts of the city. But you'll spot multifamily buildings dating from the 1950s and later on the neighborhood's main arterials, including Fulton and State. Many apartments are also available in two-family houses.

Groceries & Shopping

Old Brooklyn has several old-world specialty food markets, all of them locally owned and worth visiting even if you don't end up living here. The Sausage Shoppe, 4501 Memphis Ave., has been open since 1938, stuffing and curing its own sausages, bacon and other meat products. It was featured in the Cleveland episode of *Anthony Bourdain, No Reservations* in 2007.

Gentile's Imported Italian Food, 4464 Broadview Rd., sells delicious cheese, pasta and sauces. They also run an in-store deli and make popular pizzas. (Their name is pronounced "gen-TILL-ees.") And you can buy homemade bread and pastry at the unpretentious Michael's Bakery, 4478 Broadview Rd. Memphis Bakery, 6100 Memphis Ave., also has a loyal following. Kobawoo Oriental Food Market, 4847 Pearl Rd., sells Pacific Rim foods with an emphasis on Korean fare.

Most residents do their main grocery shopping at the 24-hour Giant Eagle, 6300 Biddulph Rd., Brooklyn, just south of Old Brooklyn's southern boundary. This location isn't as frenetic as some of the chain's other large stores.

General grocery options within the neighborhood itself mostly disappoint. There's a new Save a Lot in the Memphis-Fulton shopping center, 4215 Fulton Rd. Just up the street is a Discount Drug Mart, 4170 Memphis Ave., with a limited grocery selection and a pharmacy. Other pharmacies in the neighborhood include Rite Aid, 2323 Broadview Rd., and Walgreens, 4265 State Rd.

You can also grow your own food at Ben Franklin Community Garden, adjacent to the Ben Franklin School at 1905 Spring Ave. It's one of the largest and oldest (founded 1929) community gardens in the city.

Not in Cleveland proper, but right on the border with Old Brooklyn, is Ridge Park Square. This huge shopping center has some big box stores like Lowe's (7327 Northcliff Ave., Brooklyn) and Bed, Bath and Beyond (4766 Ridge Rd., Brooklyn). Marc's, a wildly popular local chain offering discount groceries and sundries, also has a location here (7359 Northcliff Ave., Brooklyn). Nearby, you can also shop for some of the freshest produce in Northeast Ohio at Chuppa's Marketplace, 5640 Pearl Rd.

The proximity of shopping centers like Ridge Park Square and Steelyard Commons has wiped out many of the neighborhood's independent retailers. But a few places of note remain. The immaculate South Hills Hardware, 224 Old Brookpark Rd., is one of the best independent hardware stores in the region. Its neighbor, Richardson's Greenhouse, offers vegetable plants, annuals and perennials.

Trading Post Train Shop, 4394 Pearl Rd., is a must for lovers of toy trains, while South Hills Antique Gallery, 2010 W. Schaaf Rd., sells vintage furniture and jewelry. Jindra Floral Design is in an awesome midcentury building at 4603 Pearl Rd.

Health & Recreation

One of Old Brooklyn's best features is its proximity to parks and green space. The most visible of these is the Cleveland MetroParks Zoo, in the wooded Big Creek Valley between Fulton Parkway and Pearl Road. The zoo draws more than 1 million visitors a year, but there are also trails for residents. Adjacent to the zoo is the MetroParks' Brookside Reservation – not one of the system's more visually appealing parks, but a popular place to play baseball and picnic.

The neighborhood also has a number of pocket parks that offer picnic areas and playgrounds for kids. Loew Park, 4711 W. 32nd St., is known for its baseball diamonds. Harmody Park, at the intersection of Mayview Street and South Hills Drive, is leafier and has picnic tables. From here you can catch a brand-new hike-and-bike trail – the Treadway Connector – that leads down to Steelyard Commons and the planned route of the Towpath Trail. Even before the Towpath connection happens, the short trail offers a surprisingly peaceful retreat.

The City of Cleveland operates the free Estabrook Recreation Center, 4125 Fulton Rd., with an indoor pool, gym and some fitness classes.

Eating & Drinking Out

Lots of pizza. That's the first thing you'll notice when exploring options for eating out in Old Brooklyn. Besides Gentile's, you can take your pick among Carmino's (4728 Pearl Rd.), Don Gi's Pizzeria (2159 Broadview Rd.), Nunzio's (4478 Pearl Rd.) or Bella Pizza (4830 Memphis Ave.), to name a few. Most of these are primarily take-out joints, though Dina's Pizza & Pub (5701 Memphis Ave.) has a large dining room and pub.

There are a couple of well-known diner and family-style restaurants. These are the kinds of places you went as a kid to order fries and grilled cheese and that actually have "Family Restaurant" in their names so there's no doubt about intentions. Gabe's Family Restaurant, 2044 Broadview Rd., is popular for its cheap breakfasts and comfort food; Steve's Family Restaurant, 4457 Broadview Rd., also has Greek fare.

Even better, and certainly more famous locally, are Old Brooklyn's native sweet shops. Jack Frost Donuts, 4960 Pearl Rd., fries up more than 30 varieties of sweet dough, with flavors like key lime, banana split and peanut butter and jelly. The original Honey Hut Ice Cream Shoppe, 4674 State Rd., is another neighborhood institution.

Most of the bars in Old Brooklyn are of the shot-and-a-beer variety. The most popular are clustered along Memphis Avenue and include McG's, 6815 Memphis Ave.; Fat Guy's, 5517 Memphis Ave.; and Memphis Station Bar & Grill, 6101 Memphis Ave. There's a fun karaoke night on Fridays at Mr. Peabody's, 4967 Fulton Rd., which has a cozy 1950s-era dark-wood interior. (It also has Barack Obama and Hillary Clinton urinal targets, in case you were wondering about the owners' political leanings.)

You can do some old-school Cleveland bowling at Classic Lanes, 4231 Fulton Rd., which is tucked away underneath a strip shopping center.

A movie theater, AMC Ridge Park Square (4788 Ridge Rd., Brooklyn), shows the latest Hollywood blockbusters.

Old Brooklyn: The Once Over

Like North Collinwood, Old Brooklyn is a difficult neighborhood to grasp in one walk. The walking tour below will give you a taste of the South Hills area, as well as some local retail. For a broader view you may want to hop in a car or on a bike and check out the Cleveland MetroParks Zoo and Brookside Reservation; the nearby Brookside Drive residential area; and retail shopping along Memphis Avenue between Pearl and Fulton roads.

Start at Gentile's Imported Italian Foods, 4464 Broadview Rd., where there is usually on-street parking available.

Walk about two blocks south on Broadview, in the same direction as you walked from Gentile's to Michael's. Turn left on Tampa Avenue, a solid (and typical for the neighborhood) street of single family houses and doubles. After a block you'll come to Ben Franklin Community Garden, with the elementary school behind.

Keep walking on Tampa past Broadale until you reach South Hills Drive. This is one of the most comfortable residential streets in Old Brooklyn (and indeed in all of Cleveland). Take a right on South Hills and follow its curvy path southwest for about four blocks.

When you hit pleasant Hillcrest Avenue, take a right. A block later you'll come back to Broadview; make another right. If you have time, you can walk left down Oak Park Avenue, another pleasant residential street. Otherwise, follow Broadview for another four nondescript blocks north to return to Michael's and Gentile's. Regroup with a snack and/or coffee at either place.

CLARK-FULTON AND BROOKLYN CENTRE

Clark-Fulton and Brooklyn Centre lie between the Ohio City and Old Brooklyn neighborhoods. Both offer some nice housing at low prices, though with fewer amenities than their neighbors to the North and South.

Clark-Fulton, centered around the intersection of – shocker – Clark Avenue and Fulton Road, is the heart of Cleveland's Latino community. Stores, restaurants and churches serving this community line gap-toothed Clark Avenue. Castro Hardware, 4313 Clark Ave., is one of the last surviving independent hardware stores in the city, and has friendly staff. It's worth exploring some of the other small groceries and shops on the street.

A few remnants of the West Side's oldest Italian neighborhood also remain; Mazzone & Sons Bakery, 3519 Clark Ave., has delicious Italian pastry, while St. Rocco Church, 3205 Fulton Rd., attracts worshippers from the suburbs. Bruno's Ristorante, 2644 W. 41st St., has a fantastic patio and good food.

Some of the nicest streets in Clark-Fulton are Woodbridge and Trowbridge between W. 25th and Fulton. These have sturdy pre-World War II bungalows, some built in the Arts & Crafts style. Storer Avenue, which runs parallel to Clark, has a bad reputation for crime.

Brooklyn Centre starts around Pearl Road (the name for W. 25th Street south of I-71) and Riverside Avenue. It began as an independent Western Reserve town in the early 19th century before Cleveland engulfed it. Houses from this period of its existence still stand, and the residential architecture here is some of the best in the city. See especially Archwood Avenue, west of Pearl Road, which has stunning Italianate houses built for the old town's upper class.

Brooklyn Centre had a renaissance in the 1990s, when urban pioneers bought and restored some of its grandest houses. Since then, redevelopment has slowed, though the neighborhood still draws buyers looking for intact Victorian architecture. There is a small shopping center on Pearl Road at Denison Avenue offering a laundromat and an Aldi's grocery store, and Cleveland Public Library has a branch at 3706 Pearl Rd. Otherwise, you'll be driving for entertainment and shopping. (Highway access is excellent, though, with ramps to both I-90 and I-71 off of W. 25th St.)

SLAVIC VILLAGE

Towpath Trail

day 95/100

SLAVIC VILLAGE

Slavic Village is a huge neighborhood on the city's near East Side. It has at least two distinct parts. The northern part of the neighborhood (sometimes called North Broadway) centers around the magnificent if down-at-heel intersection of E. 55th St. and Broadway Ave. The southern part (South Broadway) centers on Fleet Avenue, a modest old streetcar corridor that once had mom-and-pop shops and bakeries – though most haven't withstood competition from national chains.

Many Cleveland neighborhoods have struggled in the wake of the foreclosure crisis, but few as much, or as publicly, as Slavic Village. The statistics are staggering. In 2007, as the crisis was coming to a head, Slavic Village was seeing as many as 200 foreclosures a month – the highest rate in the region. In 2008 and 2009, these numbers attracted a swarm of reporters bent on using the neighborhood as the poster child for stories about speculative flippers and corrupt mortgage lending practices. Stories about the neighborhood appeared in *The New York Times, The Washington Post*, CNN and NPR.

The aftershocks of the crisis are still reverberating. Today, touring the neighborhood, you'll see boarded up houses and dozens of vacant lots where houses and buildings once stood. Many of the commercial buildings that remain are vacant.

But the neighborhood's heart still beats. Slavic Village Development Corporation is one of the strongest community development corporations (CDC's) in the city, with a young staff bent on lifting the neighborhood from its current nadir. In 2011, Federal Reserve Chairman

22,225

{ population }

56/100

Slavic Village's
Walk Score

LOCATION

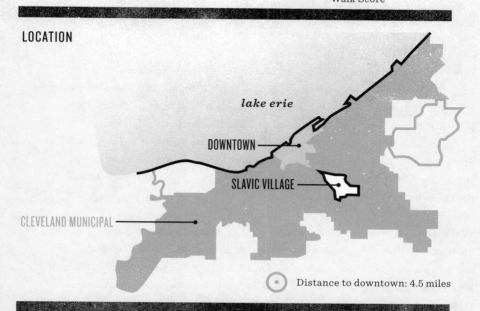

lake erie

DOWNTOWN —

SLAVIC VILLAGE —

CLEVELAND MUNICIPAL —

⊙ Distance to downtown: 4.5 miles

WHO SHOULD LIVE HERE?

Families

Professional

Artist

AMENITIES AND COMMUNITY FEATURES:

Rapid Transit	Museums	Park	Specialty Shops
Grocery Stores	Retail Shopping	Yoga	Concert Hall
Restaurants	Bookstore	Bars/Nightlife	Pharmacy
Movie Theaters	Gym	Community Garden	Farmers Market
Library	Coffee Shop	Live Theater	Sports

Ben Bernanke cited Slavic Village as one of five neighborhoods nationwide that had been most effectively dealing with foreclosure by demolishing blighted homes, reaching out to residents at risk of foreclosure, and reusing vacant land as parks, trails and gardens.

Meanwhile, plenty of committed residents remain. Some are old-timers – people whose families have lived here for generations. Others have come more recently, drawn to new infill housing and the area's proximity to both Downtown and the Towpath Trail. There's also a small artist community at the Hyacinth Lofts building.

Like Tremont, Slavic Village perches on a bluff above the Cuyahoga River. And like Tremont, the neighborhood boomed as Cleveland reached its industrial peak in the early 20th century. It drew thousands of immigrants – many of them Poles and Czechs – who could live in modest and inexpensive housing and walk to work at nearby factories. They built stunning churches, with the most impressive being the Shrine Church of St. Stanislaus, 3649 E. 65th St., grand as anything you'll see in Europe. The Slavic Village Harvest Festival, in late August, attracts families from throughout the region who have their roots here or in Slavic culture generally.

Public schools in the neighborhood include three elementary schools: the brand-new public Mound Elementary, built next to a hike and bike trail; and the older Willow School and Fullerton School. The Girls Leadership Academy is a public school for girls between kindergarten and fifth grade. Private schools include the well-regarded Cleveland Central Catholic High School and Villa Montessori, which serves kids in preschool and kindergarten. Charter schools include Washington Park Environmental Studies Academy, for high school kids.

There's a branch of the Cleveland Public Library at 7224 Broadway Ave.

Transportation

At one time, Slavic Village would have been a great place to live without a car. It has dense fabric and several small-scale commercial corridors. But the exodus of jobs and shopping to the suburbs has meant that most residents now must drive or take public transportation to meet their daily needs.

The closest Rapid station is at E. 55th St. and Bower Avenue, a particularly bleak part of the city that, for most of the neighborhood, is too far for walking. That said, all three of the main train lines pass through here, so you can connect directly to Downtown, University

Circle, the airport, Shaker Square and points east. Buses run down Broadway Avenue, Fleet Avenue and E. 55th Street.

Highway access is excellent; most of the neighborhood lies within a two-minute drive of either I-77 or I-490, which connects to I-71 and I-90 Westbound. You can reach I-480 from either of these entry points, while I-77 yields access to I-90 Eastbound.

A growing number of people bicycle in Slavic Village, either for commuting or recreation. The neighborhood has been working hard to support cyclists. The off-road Morgana Run Trail connects to the Towpath Trail and also passes by the new Mound Elementary School, new ball fields around E. 71st St. and Broadway, and the neighborhood's commercial heart at E. 55th and Broadway.

Housing

In the late 19th and early 20th centuries, developers built many of the houses in Slavic Village quickly and cheaply to accommodate floods of new immigrants. If there's a silver lining to the foreclosure debacle, it's that the neighborhood has an opportunity to clear the flimsiest of these to make way for better housing when the market rebounds (see box, p. 91).

But fine Victorians and doubles also exist. Some of the nicest blocks are around the Shrine Church of St. Stanislaus, at E. 65th St. and Forman Avenue. There are also some new infill townhouses here. Other fine old streets include Ottawa Road and Indiana Avenue, both off E. 71st Street.

The neighborhood also saw some infill development in the 1990s and 2000s. One example is Mill Creek Run, at the neighborhood's southern tip and adjacent to Mill Creek Park and Trail, which connects to the 100-mile Ohio & Erie Towpath Trail. While this development tries perhaps a bit too hard to mimic a suburban subdivision, more recent examples mesh better with the historic fabric. The Cloisters, for example, is a townhouse development lining E. 65th Street, near St. Stanislaus. There are plans for a new townhouse development near the campus of Third Federal Bank, at E. 71st and Aetna Road.

Artists may want to check out the Hyacinth Lofts, 2998 E. 63rd St., in a former Board of Education building. The building, tucked in the northernmost corner of the neighborhood, is now home to filmmakers and musicians. (The building offers a common video screening area and rehearsal space.)

Groceries & Shopping

Slavic Village has several discount grocers, including Bi-Rite (6405 Fleet Ave.), Save A Lot (6501 Harvard Ave.) and Aldi's (6711 Broadway Ave.). All emphasize processed and frozen food over fresh produce. But there's also a more complete Dave's Supermarket at 7422 Harvard Ave. The Broadway Farmers' Market brings locally grown food to the neighborhood on Mondays from 4 to 7 p.m., June through October. The market happens at the intersection of Broadway and Baxter avenues.

You can also grow your own produce at one of the neighborhood's community gardens. One of the oldest and largest is Morganic Garden, at E. 65th St. and Kenyon Ave.; others include Union Community Garden at E. 74th St. and Union Ave.; and Regent Garden, at E. 70th St. and Temple Ave.

There are some wonderful old-world meat markets and bakeries. Seven Roses, 6301 Fleet Ave., bakes its own bread and sells a selection of homemade Polish cookies, pierogi and potato pancakes. Imported Polish dry goods are also on offer. The airy, tin-ceilinged interior also has a small dine-in area. Krusinski's Finest Meats, 6300 Heisley Ave., is famous not only for its meats but its pierogi. Neighbors also love R & K Sausages, 7700 Harvard Ave., next to the Dave's Supermarket. The charming C & H Gertrude Bakery, hidden away at 6506 Gertrude Ave., sells pastry and breads.

Discount Drug Mart, 3889 E. 71st St., also has a limited selection of groceries but is mostly a pharmacy and general store. Other pharmacies in the neighborhood include CVS, 6301 Harvard Ave.; Rite Aid, 7109 Harvard Ave.; and Walgreens, 6410 Broadway Ave.

Health & Recreation

Neighborhood leaders have been working hard to make Slavic Village a place known for "active living," where residents can live healthfully without needing to join a gym. Their efforts have led so far to the Morgana Run Trail, which connects to both the Towpath and neighborhood amenities; new ball fields at Broadway and E. 71st St.; and a series of programs to encourage residents to walk and bike to school and work. A private developer is considering opening a huge indoor bicycle track – known as a velodrome – on a nine-acre former hospital site at Broadway and McBride avenues.

There are also several parks. Mill Creek Park deserves special mention. It offers walking and jogging trails through a wooded ravine, and its star attraction is Mill Creek Falls, at 48 feet the tallest waterfall in Cuyahoga County. From Mill Creek Trail you can bicycle 100 miles south on the Towpath Trail through the Cuyahoga Valley National Park and beyond.

The free neighborhood recreation center is Stella Walsh, 7345 Broadway Ave., which has a pool and a few fitness classes. The Boys and Girls Club of Cleveland, 6114 Broadway Ave., offers activities and sports for kids between the ages of 6 and 18.

The 59-acre Washington Reservation straddles Slavic Village and the neighboring suburb of Newburgh Heights. The park, around Fleet Avenue and Washington Park Boulevard, offers a short multipurpose trail and some picnic areas. Its star attraction is the Washington Golf Learning Center, which uses golf to teach life skills to neighborhood kids.

Eating & Drinking Out

The best known restaurant in the neighborhood is The Red Chimney, 6501 Fleet Ave. This place defines "greasy spoon diner," with cheap breakfasts that cost less than $3.

The New Harvard Inn, 4055 E. 71st St., serves Eastern European food (think pierogi) at cheap prices.

There's a nice coffee shop, Shipley's Coffee House, 3664 E. 65th St., across from St. Stanislaus.

Slavic Village: The Once Over

Slavic Village is huge. But you can get a flavor of the neighborhood by starting at the Morganic Gardens, a large community garden at the intersection of E. 65th Street and Kenyon Avenue. (Easy street parking nearby.) On the other side of E. 65th Street are some new ballfields. This was the old Warszawa district, settled by Polish immigrants in the late 19th century.

Walk South on E. 65th Street, with the Gardens to your right. If you're a big meat-eater, you can take a small detour to your right down Heisley Avenue to visit Krusinski's Finest Meat Products, 6300 Heisley Ave.

Continuing south, you'll pass some infill townhouses and then the magnificent Shrine Church of St. Stanislaus, at the intersection of E. 65th and Forman Avenue. If the church is open, be sure to peek inside.

Turn left down Forman Avenue. This isn't one of the neighborhood's premier streets, but the well-kept houses will give you a sense of the older housing stock in the area. You'll pass well-regarded Cleveland Central Catholic High School on your left.

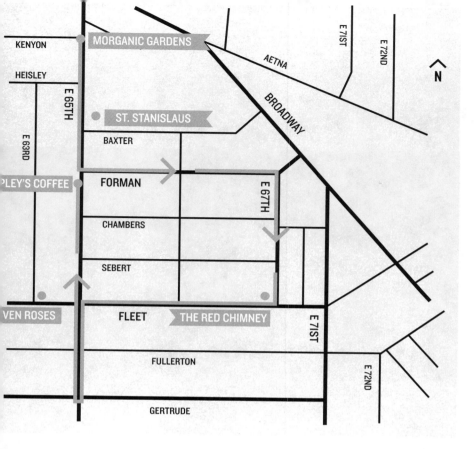

At tree-lined E. 67th Street, turn right and walk for three blocks. At Fleet Avenue, turn right. In a block you'll pass The Red Chimney Restaurant, 6501 Fleet Ave., the neighborhood's famous greasy spoon diner. Keep walking on Fleet until you reach the Slavic Village Bi-Rite, 6405 Fleet Ave. A few doors past Bi-Rite is Seven Roses Deli, 6301 Fleet Ave.; you could stop in here for a sandwich or pastry on your return trip if you'd like.

Cross Fleet Avenue on E. 65th Street. Walk two blocks south until you reach Gertrude Avenue. Just east of the intersection, at 6506 Gertrude Ave., is C&H Gertrude Bakery – well worth a stop.

From Gertrude Bakery, retrace your steps back up E. 65th Street to Fleet Avenue. Continue north on E. 65th Street across Fleet Avenue. On your left will be some new infill townhouses. These are part of The Cloisters development, spearheaded by St. Stanislaus Pulaski Franciscan Community Development Corporation and Third Federal Bank.

As you re-approach St. Stanislaus, you'll see Shipley's Coffee House, 3664 E. 65th St., a good place to close out your tour.

UNIVERSITY CIRCLE

—— —  —— —

LITTLE ITALY

SEVERANCE HALL

Severance Hall

day 93/100

UNIVERSITY CIRCLE AND LITTLE ITALY

—

University Circle (the neighborhood got its name from an old streetcar turnaround that no longer exists) wasn't always the institutional mecca it became in the 1970s and 1980s. Prior to those decades, it had plenty of residential side streets flanking cultural stalwarts such as Case Western Reserve University, University Hospitals, the Cleveland Institute of Art (CIA), the Cleveland Institute of Music (CIM) and the Cleveland Museum of Art. For art students and music students, CIA and CIM are near the tops of their respective fields.

But when some of those institutions wanted to expand starting in the 1960s, they began to buy up formerly residential areas to erect new buildings and parking garages. A nonprofit organization, University Circle Inc., was even formed to aid in the process, helping to buy and hold land so the institutions could grow. (UCI now performs a much broader function, seeking to make the neighborhood more amenable for businesses and residents alike.) As in so many places in Cleveland, tense race relations also came into play. Some of the demolitions cleared black neighborhoods around the heart of the Circle.

The result was that University Circle became an impressive but rather lifeless place. It has some of the best academic, cultural and medical institutions in the world, and is Northeast Ohio's second largest employment hub after Downtown. Yet comparatively few people now live here.

But that's beginning to change. Developers, with assistance from the City and University Circle Inc., have begun to understand the huge pent-up demand for residential options

7,906
{ population }

LOCATION

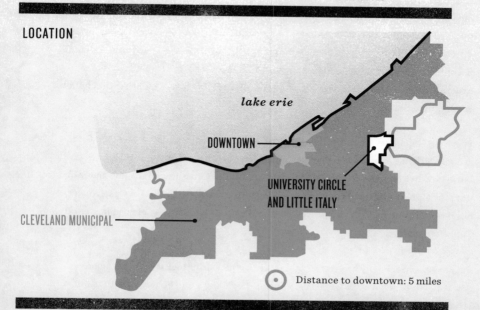

lake erie

DOWNTOWN —

UNIVERSITY CIRCLE
AND LITTLE ITALY

CLEVELAND MUNICIPAL —

⊙ Distance to downtown: 5 miles

WHO SHOULD LIVE HERE?

| Student | Families | Professional | Empty nester | Artist | No car needed |

AMENITIES AND COMMUNITY FEATURES:

Rapid Transit	Museums	Park	Specialty Shops
Grocery Stores	Retail Shopping	Yoga	Concert Hall
Restaurants	Bookstore	Bars/Nightlife	Pharmacy
Movie Theaters	Gym	Community Garden	Farmers Market
Library	Coffee Shop	Live Theater	Sports

in the neighborhood. New townhouses and apartment buildings are rising along Euclid Avenue between E. 105th and the East Cleveland border, catering to the many people who want to be able to walk to the area's museums, Severance Hall (home of The Cleveland Orchestra) and gorgeous Rockefeller Park.

The largest new development is Uptown, around the intersection of Euclid Avenue and Ford Drive (which turns into Mayfield on the south side of Euclid). Two new buildings, designed by Stanley Saitowitz, have broken ground on some former parking lots and will offer apartments, stores and restaurants starting in 2012. The Cleveland Museum of Contemporary Art is also building a new home here, a drunken Rubik's Cube of a structure designed by starchitect Farshid Moussavi of London. It will be her first building in the United States.

These developments are filling in blank spaces that will help connect University Circle to Little Italy, a tiny enclave less than a mile from the heart of University Circle. Little Italy lies immediately south of University Circle, across Euclid Avenue, but is divided from the Circle by railroad tracks and parking lots. It attracts students at Case Western Reserve University and the institutes of art and music – and still has a sizeable, if declining, Italian population.

But professionals, empty nesters and others are now clamoring to live in the neighborhood, too. It's easy to see why. Little Italy is one of Cleveland's most charming districts. It has brick streets and wedding-cake churches and fat men tumbling out of cheerful restaurants. Situated on a gentle hillside leading to neighboring Cleveland Heights, it may be this country's closest approximation of an actual Italian hill town outside of San Francisco's North Hill.

Historically, Little Italy had a reputation for being unwelcoming – some say hostile – to blacks. This is beginning to fade, but you may still encounter anti-black sentiment among some longer-term residents and merchants.

Little Italy sprang up in the early 20th century to house Italian stonemasons and their families. Many of the masons built headstones and ornamentation for the graves of wealthy industrialists at nearby Lakeview Cemetery. The descendants of many of these families are long gone, having traveled up Mayfield Road to suburbs like South Euclid and Mayfield Heights. But they continue to own most of the area's real estate and its many shops and restaurants. Houses for sale are rare, leading to projects like 27 Coltman, a high-end townhouse development on Little Italy's eastern edge.

Transportation

Public transit is among the best in Cleveland. Two Red Line Rapid stations bookend the neighborhood. One is at Cedar Avenue near Murray Hill Road, at the southwest end of Little Italy. The other is at Euclid Avenue and E. 120th St., on the northeast end. The Regional Transit Authority has plans to move the latter to near the intersection of Mayfield and Euclid, making it more convenient to the heart of both University and Little Italy.

The Health Line, the "bus rapid transit" line that connects University Circle with Downtown, plies Euclid Avenue. It runs at least every 15 minutes and will get you Downtown in about 20. There are traditional buses on Cedar Avenue and Mayfield Road, connecting with Downtown and the suburbs of Cleveland Heights, South Euclid and beyond. Another bus, the #48, takes a circuitous route to Shaker Square.

University Circle and Little Italy are great walking neighborhoods, built at the scale of pedestrians rather than cars. Bicycling is something of a challenge in Little Italy because of narrow streets and grade changes, but it's certainly doable. Once you cross north of Euclid to University Circle, the way is flat and easy. Euclid Avenue has dedicated bike lanes going most of the way Downtown. There are also bike lanes through Rockefeller Park, which is one of the loveliest green spaces in the city.

Housing

Much of the existing housing in University Circle and Little Italy serves students. As such, many of the apartments here are not maintained at the highest levels of repair. You can find dozens of listings geared to students on Craig's List, and by walking the surrounding streets.

If you're looking to put down roots here, your best options are the Murray Hill Condos, loft apartments and condos in an old schoolhouse; the new townhouses at 27 Coltman, or Circle 118; and the upcoming Uptown project. The area institutions have acquired most of the historic housing in the Circle itself, but you can still find beautiful old houses for sale on Wade Park Avenue and Ashbury Avenue east of E. 105th Street in Glenville (see p. 140).

Park Lane Villa, 10510 Park Lane, is a beautifully restored old apartment building on E. 105th Street north of Chester Avenue – somewhat removed from many neighborhood attractions but still worth a look.

Little Italy

day 29/100

The best part of living in University Circle and Little Italy is that you can walk to some of the most venerated museums and cultural institutions in the world. Chief among these are The Cleveland Museum of Art and Severance Hall, home of The Cleveland Orchestra. The Cleveland Cinematheque is also here. If you're a junky for high-culture, University Circle is the place to live. For more information about the individual institutions, see p. 210.

Groceries & Shopping

As of 2011, the only place to buy groceries within the neighborhood itself was Murray Hill Market, 2072 Murray Hill Rd. With its cracked tile floors and tasteful selection of pastas, cheeses and (very) limited produce, the place feels straight off a street corner in Rome. You can also buy delicious sandwiches here, and pints of Jeni's Ice Cream – an Ohio delicacy.

A Contanstino's grocery store will open in the Uptown development in 2012, but major grocery trips will likely find you heading up the hill to Cleveland Heights. Zagara's, about three miles away at 1940 Lee Rd., is the best option. It's an independently owned supermarket with a great produce section and plenty of organics. (If you're feeling spendy and have a car, Whole Foods' local flagship store is in University Heights at 13998 Cedar Rd., about four miles from University Circle and Little Italy.)

You can buy fresh-baked bread and pastries at both Corbo's Bakery (12210 Mayfield Rd.) and Presti's Bakery (12101 Mayfield Rd.). Presti's also serves as a coffee shop; see below.

The Murray Hill Schoolhouse, 2026 Murray Hill Rd., has a few upscale boutique stores, including the gift shop Juma Gallery, and the women's clothing outpost Anne van H. Boutique. Little Italy Wines, 12414 Mayfield Rd., is a microscopic but well-stocked wine store with a helpful staff. A larger beer and wine store is Circle Convenience, at 11313 Euclid Ave. Mayfield Smoke Shop, 12307 Mayfield Rd., has tobacco and chewing gum and a cast of surly but charming neighborhood curmudgeons. There are also a dozen or more art galleries, nice but not very useful for everyday use.

Other types of shopping within the neighborhood are limited – though again, this will change when Uptown comes online. The development is slated to have a Barnes & Noble bookstore and a CVS Pharmacy, along with independent restaurants.

From the center of Little Italy, it's about a mile up Mayfield Road – a pleasant walk – to Coventry Road in Cleveland Heights. This historic street offers some of the best independent shopping in the region (see p. 194).

Cleveland Museum of Art

day 81/100

Health & Recreation

Anyone can join Case Western Reserve University's gym, 1-2-1 Fitness Center (2130 Adelbert Rd.). It operates as a standalone facility, with the expected slate of spinning and yoga classes. (No swimming pool, though.) If you're not a student, don't worry about not fitting in; the place is popular with people of all ages.

Alta House (12510 Mayfield Rd.,) is a kind of Italian-American community center. It offers a free, barebones gym operated by the city, and outdoor bocce courts. You can also take Italian lessons here; check the website for details or call 216-421-1536.

The Yoga Room (2026 Murray Hill Rd., Room 210,) is a small but airy yoga studio inside the Murray Hill Schoolhouse. It offers classes of all styles and levels, at some of the most affordable prices in town – $10 for a drop-in class.

The neighborhood's two largest green spaces – Rockefeller Park and Lakeview Cemetery – are among the loveliest places in Northeast Ohio.

Rockefeller Park follows Martin Luther King Boulevard all the way north to Lake Erie. The 200-acre park, designed by a protégée of Frederick Law Olmstead, was set aside as green space in 1897. For all its beauty, though, it can seem eerily empty of people. This is partly due to the heavy vehicular traffic it handles – MLK is the most popular route from University Circle to I-90. But tense race relations haven't helped, either.

The neighborhoods above the park are Hough and Glenville, which suffered race riots in the 1960s (see p. 14). Only recently has this legacy begun to recede. University Circle Inc. and the nonprofit ParkWorks have completed a new strategic plan for the park that will make it more inviting for pedestrians.

Rockefeller Park's best-known feature is its dozens of cultural gardens, each honoring one of Cleveland's ethnic groups. Most of the original gardens were installed before World War II, and represent the predominant immigrant groups of that time – Italians, Irish, Hungarians, Polish. But new interest in the gardens grew in the 2000s, and more recent immigrant groups (Indian, Azeri, Uzbek, Armenian) have completed gardens of their own. The best way to visit them is on foot or on bicycle. MLK Boulevard has dedicated bicycle lanes on both sides, but avoid them during rush hour. East Boulevard, which runs parallel to and above MLK, offers the best views of some of the gardens, and its east side is lined by some of the grandest mansions and apartment houses in the city.

Lake View Cemetery, dedicated in 1869, straddles Cleveland, East Cleveland and Cleveland Heights. You can enter the 200-acre cemetery from Mayfield Road, near the border of Cleveland and Cleveland Heights; or from Euclid Avenue and E. 121st Street. Here are the graves of famous Clevelanders like John D. Rockefeller and Marcus Hanna, many with ostentatious ornamentation and statuary. The most famous site in the cemetery is the monument and grave of President James Garfield, in a stone tower at the top of a hill. You can climb a spiral staircase to the top, taking in stunning views of University Circle, Downtown and Lake Erie.

Eating & Drinking Out
Surprise: Restaurant options in Little Italy are almost entirely Italian. But a couple of newcomers, at opposite ends of the price spectrum, are adding variety to the neighborhood's culinary landscape. Teahouse Noodles (2218 Murray Hill Rd.) serves mix-and-match rice and noodle bowls with delicious sauces for under $10. Club Isabella (2175 Cornell Rd.), has New American cuisine in one of the city's loveliest dining rooms – and with a patio to boot.

Favorite Italian places are Trattoria on the Hill (12207 Mayfield Rd.), with portions so large they could feed you for a week (especially good are the gnocchi and eggplant parmesan); Maxi's (12113 Mayfield Rd.), which doubles as a hip bar; and La Dolce Vita (12112 Mayfield Rd.). Mama Santa's (12305 Mayfield Rd.) is Cleveland's most beloved pizzeria. The pies are tasty and surprisingly cheap; the crowds spill out the door on Saturday nights.

Washington Place Bistro (2203 Cornell Rd.) replaced the old Barricelli Inn with an updated menu of New American cuisine. It's still the most upscale place to eat in the neighborhood.

There's greater variety – but fewer overall choices – down in University Circle. Indian Flame (11623 Euclid Ave.) serves no-frills but delicious South Indian cuisine. Falafel Café (11365 Euclid Ave.) has cheap Middle Eastern fare. On the pricier side are Sergio's (1903 Ford Dr.), which has a nice patio and New American food, and L'Albatros (11401 Bellflower Rd.), with a French menu.

Bars, in the strictest sense, are few and far between. Little Italy has tiny Lounge Leo, 2161 Murray Hill Rd. The Euclid Tavern (11625 Euclid Ave.) was famous from the 1960s through the 1990s as a punk-rock mecca. New owners renovated the place in 2008, some say to the point of sterilization. The Barking Spider Tavern (11310 Juniper Rd.) is a folk and blues joint that's been around as long as anyone can remember.

Reflecting the large number of students, Little Italy and University Circle have no shortage of coffee shops. In Little Italy, there's quirky Algebra Teahouse (2136 Murray Hill Rd.), with its odd but pleasant forest-like interior. Presti's (12101 Murray Hill Rd.) is a bakery and coffee shop that's always packed. It serves excellent gelato from La Gelateria in Cleveland Heights. University Circle offers The Coffee House, 11300 Bellflower Rd., in a repurposed mansion, and two Starbucks shops – one at 11302 Euclid Ave. and another at 1656 E. 115th St. with more limited hours and serving mostly Case students.

Look for more bars and restaurants to emerge when Uptown goes live in 2012.

University Circle & Little Italy: The Once Over

The neighborhood is active all the time because of the museums and university, but try to come when classes are in session (September through May) to see what the neighborhood's like with its full population of students.

Start at the geographic and cultural heart of the neighborhood: The Cleveland Museum of Art, 11150 East Blvd. If you're arriving by car, there's a parking garage here, or you can find metered parking on Wade Oval or East Boulevard. If you have limited time, just grab a gallery map and see the building – otherwise the artistic distractions could keep you from seeing the rest of the neighborhood.

At the Art Museum's rear entrance is Wade Oval. Arranged around this large lawn are the Natural History Museum and the Botanical Garden. Directly across East from the Art Museum is the Cleveland Institute of Art, home of the Cinematheque. Enter the building if you want a film schedule. Look to your left, where you can make out the contemporary white façade of the Cleveland Institute of Music. The Western Reserve Historical Society and the Crawford Auto-Aviation Museum are beyond.

If you're interested in big old houses, detour north along East 108th Street to Wade Park Avenue. This boulevard forms the unofficial northern border of University Circle; further north is Glenville (see box, p. 140). Some of the houses on Wade Park are owned by nearby institutions, and host students, visiting doctors and artists. But most are privately owned. The blocks between here and Ashbury, parallel to Wade Park and a block north, also have some nice houses, many in need of TLC.

Walk South on East Boulevard, with the Art Museum to your right. You'll see Wade Lagoon below, usually cacophonous with the quacking of Canada geese. On your left is Severance Hall, built in 1930, home of the Cleveland Orchestra. If the front door, facing on Euclid, is open, take a peek inside at the gaudy art deco lobby.

At the intersection of East Boulevard and Euclid Ave., turn left. On both sides of the street are the buildings of Case Western Reserve University and its affiliated hospital system, University Hospitals. Keep going until you reach the three-way intersection of Euclid, Ford and Mayfield. On the Ford side, to your left, you can walk a block north to Hessler Road if you like. The street has nice old attached houses and, at its far end, the only surviving wood block street in Cleveland. Keep your eyes peeled for "For Rent" signs if you're interested in living here.

Cross Euclid to Mayfield Road. At the corner, the Museum of Contemporary Art's new building is rising. If you look East down Euclid, you'll see the mid-rise buildings of Uptown. Beyond them is the E. 120th St. Rapid station.

Stick to Mayfield and walk past a dispiriting surface parking lot to your left. On the right is the Italianate Cozad-Bates House, an important stop on the Underground Railroad in the 19th century. Efforts are underway to restore the house and open it as a museum.

You'll come to a dingy overpass as you keep walking on Mayfield; this holds the Red Line Rapid tracks and will be the site of the new Mayfield Rapid station whenever RTA gets

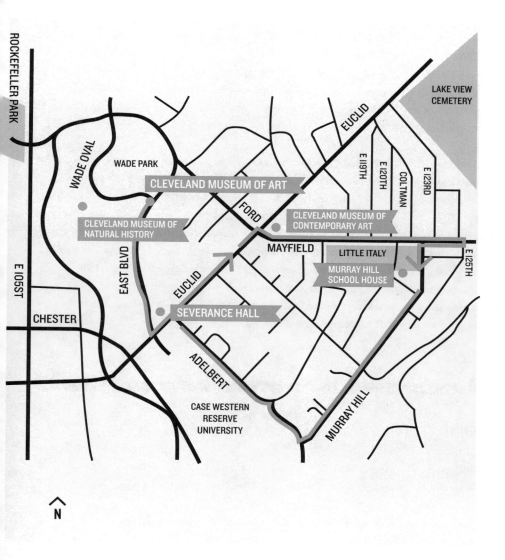

the money together. Cross underneath and you'll come to Little Italy's main drag along Mayfield Road, heralded by the imposing Our Lady of the Rosary Church.

Wander up Mayfield to Alta House, at E. 125th St., checking out any shops or bakeries that float your fancy. At Alta House, note the bocce courts and tour the very basic Rec Center if you like. If you have time, walk uphill on Mayfield Road about a quarter mile to Lake View Cemetery, one of the city's star attractions.

Otherwise, double back downhill to Murray Hill Road, still paved in red brick, and turn left. You'll pass Murray Hill Schoolhouse, now condos and rentals. Contact the Murray Hill Condominiums (216-421-9000) if you'd like to arrange a viewing. In the front building are a few gift and clothing stores. Continue down Murray Hill until you get to Murray Hill Market, 2072 Murray Hill Rd. Stop here to check out where you'll shop in a pinch or for Italian specialty items.

Keep going on Murray Hill, noting "For Rent" signs and phone numbers, all the way to Adelbert Road. (A few blocks further is the University-Cedar Rapid Station.) You'll pass more restaurants, including Teahouse Noodles.

Turn right on Adelbert, passing more University Hospitals buildings. On your left will be 1-2-1 Fitness Center, 2130 Adelbert Rd. If you're into working out, check inside for the class schedule and a tour. Continue down Adelbert to Euclid. You'll see Severance Hall and the Art Museum; cross Euclid Avenue to East Boulevard to return to your starting point. If you'd like a place to unwind, try The Coffee House, 11300 Bellflower Rd., or (for drinks) the Barking Spider Tavern, 11310 Juniper Rd.

GLENVILLE

Glenville borders University Circle to the North, with Wade Park Avenue as the unofficial border. Its western boundary is East Boulevard and Rockefeller Park (see above).

The neighborhood was once solidly middle and upper-middle class. After World War II, its primarily Jewish residents began moving to the suburbs and the neighborhood became predominantly black by 1960. In 1968, riots broke out following a shootout between Cleveland police and a black neighborhood group, giving Glenville a reputation for violence.

The past 50 years have seen steady disinvestment. The recent foreclosure crisis has been particularly traumatic here, with many houses now vacant and boarded – some demolished.

But Glenville still has many grand houses in good repair. Its premier residential street is East Boulevard. The blocks north of Superior Avenue are lined with stunning houses built before 1930, almost all in pristine condition. South of Superior are some stately apartment buildings that look like they got lost on their way to Boston. These are mostly co-ops. The neighborhood development corporation is renovating one or two of them to capitalize on demand for housing in and around University Circle. (For more information, contact the Famicos Foundation, 216-791-6476.)

East 105th Street between Euclid and St. Clair avenues is Glenville's historic main drag. It has faded in the face of falling population and new retail trends, with surface parking beginning to outnumber buildings. But much remains. Especially impressive is the former Amshe Emeth Synagogue at 1117 E. 105th St., now Cory United Methodist Church. Further south toward University Circle, at the intersection of E. 105th Street and Ansel Road, Park Synagogue is another impressive structure. It still hosts ceremonies during Jewish high holy days but the congregation has moved to Beachwood. Case Western Reserve University bought the building in 2010 and will use it as a performing arts center.

Some of the side streets off E. 105th remain well-tended; others are pockmarked with weedy lots and empty houses. The houses are cruise-ship big, built during an era of cheap energy. In fact, the size of the houses in Glenville – once one of its selling points – has become a liability in the face of escalating heating bills.

Perhaps no place in Cleveland displays as much faded grandeur as Glenville. It's easy to tour its streets and yearn in sepia tones for lost bakeries and bustle. But with demand growing for housing in and around University Circle – and with Rockefeller Park likely to get a makeover in coming years – Glenville may be poised for rejuvenation.

Urban Farms

day 68/100

Wade Lagoon, outside the Cleveland Museum of Art

day 4/100

Edgewater Park

day 65/100

EDGEWATER

EDGEWATER

Though it's entirely in the City of Cleveland, Edgewater has an uptown, streetcar-suburb feel reminiscent of the Main Line suburbs of Philadelphia. In fact, the neighborhood grew up in the 1910s and 1920s around a streetcar route (now long gone) along Clifton Avenue.

Edgewater is one of the most stable areas of the city. With gracious old houses and big trees on generous lots, it's never lost its luster among professionals, especially those who want easy access to downtown (only 3-4 miles away) but with a bit of leafiness on the side. True to the neighborhood's name, Lake Erie is also close by. Edgewater Park, reachable from West Boulevard, has a beach, walking paths and breezy picnic areas overlooking downtown and the water. The most expensive houses – along Edgewater and Cliff drives – perch on a bluff above the lake and have sweeping views of blue and sky.

The borders of the neighborhood are roughly West Boulevard to the East; W. 117th Street to the West; and Lake Erie to the North. The southern boundary is fuzzy. Edgewater proper seems to end at Baltic Avenue and the train tracks, but just a block south is Detroit Avenue. There's a fairly active commercial district on Detroit between W. 110th and W. 117th streets, with a coffee shop, an all-night diner and the city's most popular costume shop (Chelsea's – see below). Generally, the closer you get to the lake, the more upscale your neighbors will be.

Gay men and women have been an important – if understated – presence in Edgewater for decades. Many of the gay folks here are older and coupled, meaning that the restaurants and bars tend to be gay-friendly, but there's hardly a raging singles scene. Edgewater does have a few specifically gay hangouts, including the bar/club Twist Social Club, 11633

7,633

{ population }

68/100

Edgewater's Walk Score

LOCATION

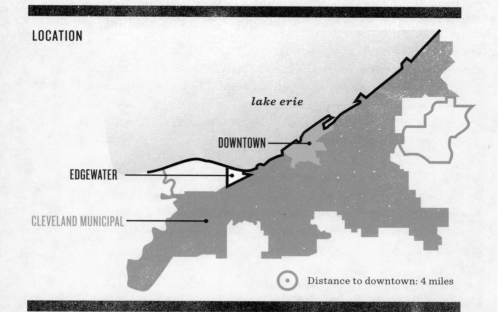

lake erie

DOWNTOWN

EDGEWATER

CLEVELAND MUNICIPAL

Distance to downtown: 4 miles

WHO SHOULD LIVE HERE?

Student

Families

Professional

Empty nester

No car needed

AMENITIES AND COMMUNITY FEATURES:

Rapid Transit	Museums	Park	Specialty Shops
Grocery Stores	Retail Shopping	Yoga	Concert Hall
Restaurants	Bookstore	Bars/Nightlife	Pharmacy
Movie Theaters	Gym	Community Garden	Farmers Market
Library	Coffee Shop	Live Theater	Sports

Clifton Blvd., and a few older bars on Detroit Avenue. Truffles, a gay coffee shop at 11122 Clifton Blvd., seems to cycle in and out of being every few months; at present its doors are closed. (For more on gay life in Cleveland, see p. 230.)

The coupling of easy access to Downtown and cheap rents make Edgewater a popular choice for students at Cleveland State University who don't want to live Downtown or can't afford it.

Transportation

The West Boulevard Rapid station, near West Boulevard and Detroit Avenue, is within walking distance of the eastern part of the neighborhood. The area around the station can feel dicey at night, but for regular commuting it's perfectly safe. There's another station at W. 117th St. and Madison Avenue, but it's far from the heart of Edgewater. You could use it, however, as a park-and-ride.

Many people who live on and around Clifton Boulevard rely on the fast 55X bus to get them to and from Downtown. The bus ambles down Clifton but then hops on the Shoreway at West Boulevard, where it picks up warp speed (for a bus) until reaching the city center. Detroit Avenue also has buses, though they are not speedy by any stretch of the imagination.

Bicyclists have a few ways to traverse the neighborhood. Clifton Boulevard is busy but wide and flat, so it's usually not too scary to pedal there; Lake Avenue is quieter and may be more pleasant.

The closest highway is the West Shoreway. You can enter from either Clifton Boulevard or Lake Avenue around West Boulevard. From there, it's five minutes to Downtown, where you can pick up any of the interstate highways going East or South (I-90, I-71 and I-77). Traveling West is less convenient. You can pick up I-90 around W. 117th St. north of Lorain Avenue, but for I-71 South you have to go far South and West to W. 130th and Bellaire.

Housing

Edgewater has one of the most diverse housing mixes in the city. On Detroit, Clifton and Lake, you'll find a good number of apartment buildings and a few mid-rise condo developments – some lovely and old, some tacky and more recent. Rental rates in these buildings are very affordable, ranging from $400 for a studio or 1-bedroom to $700 or so for a 2-bedroom. These rates typically include heat, a huge plus. You can buy condos for less than $100,000 in the 1980s-era buildings on Lake.

The side streets south of Clifton, meanwhile, are dominated by big single-family houses and doubles. Most date from the 1910s and later. Some of these are owner-occupied, but many are for rent. Rates, again, range from $400 to $700, though in houses you're likely to pay for heat separately. Sales prices are typically around $100,000 for a single-family or double, though the foreclosure crisis has created a glut of housing and some bargain-basement prices. The farther south you're willing to go, the cheaper the prices, but be aware of the expected trade-offs in convenience and safety.

Lake and Edgewater avenues have grand homes in stone and brick, but also some post-World War II ranches and Cape Cods. The prices are noticeably higher here. Expect to pay $250,000 and up even for a modest ranch.

Groceries & Shopping

For convenience food shopping, there's Constantino's Market at 11022 Clifton Blvd. The grocery selection is only a notch above that of a gas-and-go, though the wine and beer choices are good.

For major trips, you'll be traveling a few miles south to the huge and chaotic Giant Eagle at 3050 W. 117th St. There's a smaller, quieter Giant Eagle in Lakewood, at 14100 Detroit Ave. Nature's Bin, at the West edge of Lakewood, is a wonderful nonprofit grocery with organic produce and health food (see p. 200).

There's a CVS Pharmacy at 11706 Clifton Blvd., just across the Lakewood border.

Edgewater has some of the best vintage clothes and costume shopping in Cleveland. Most of the stores are a step above thrift stores – that is, shop owners have curated the selection to some extent, so you'll spend less time riffling through five-year-old Browns t-shirts. Chelsea's Costumes, 1412 W. 116th St., has an enormous selection of men's and women's styles from the 1940s onward. The store also rents and sells Halloween costumes. Across the street, The Cleveland Shop (11606 Detroit Ave.) is smaller but less cramped than Chelsea's. Flower Child, 11508 Clifton Blvd., has two floors of vintage clothing as well as furniture and knick-knacks.

If you're looking for old toys and games, check out Big Fun, 11512 Clifton Blvd. This is the West Side outpost of the original Coventry Road location. A new, gay-themed novelty store called Torso has opened next door at 11520 Clifton Blvd.

The Bent Crayon (11600 Detroit Ave.) is an independent record store that has been beating the odds for a good 15 years. You can find vintage records here as well as new stuff that meets music-snob standards for obscurity.

You can buy men's clothing of the corporate variety at Christophier Custom Clothiers (9308 Clifton Blvd.), a stand-alone store at the end of the West Shoreway. Owner Maurice Christopher also does fittings for custom shirts and suits.

There's a pet store, Pet-Tique, at 10906 Clifton Blvd. It has an array of dog and cat food and supplies, and hosts a monthly "Yappie Hour" where pet owners can eat pizza, drink wine and let their pooches sniff each other's nether regions.

Health & Recreation

The star natural attraction of Edgewater is Lake Erie, and the best way to access the lake is via Edgewater State Park. The park is the most-visited state park in Ohio, and you'll see why when you take in the unforgettable views of both the lake and Downtown. Here you'll find jogging and bicycle trails and a beach. For private boaters, there's a marina.

You can go swimming at Edgewater beach for most of the summer, especially as the water warms after July 4. Be forewarned, though, that while Lake Erie has gotten much cleaner since its nadir in the 1970s, it's far from pristine. Industrial chemicals aren't the main problem; it's raw sewage, which can wash into the lake during major storm events. (Pause while you gag.) Park administrators monitor water pollution levels throughout the swimming season and, if levels aren't safe, will post warning signs. You can also check water quality online at http://publicapps.odh.ohio.gov/BeachGuardPublic.

Surfing – yes, surfing – is also gaining in popularity. Lake Erie waves aren't as awesome as those on the coasts, but in the winter they're high enough to give you a short ride. Cleveland surfing is strictly a cold-weather affair; in the summer the lake is too placid. So you'll need to wear a full-body suit to keep warm. You can visit a popular blog, http://thesewerpipe.blogspot.com/, for more information.

At the other end of the adventure spectrum is Anytime Fitness, 11517 Clifton Blvd., a 24-hour gym with the usual assortment of classes and weight machines.

Be Studios (10404 Clifton Blvd.) offers a grab bag of massage and body treatments.

Eating & Dining Out

Edgewater doesn't have as many restaurants or bars as places like Tremont or Ohio City. What's here tends to be less flashy than in either of those neighborhoods, serving more as neighborhood hang-outs than as destinations.

The Diner on Clifton, 11637 Clifton Blvd., may be the most fun place to eat. It draws a mix of gay and straight clientele for comfort food like burgers and macaroni and cheese. Papa Nick's, 11534 Clifton Blvd., has above-average pizza and a friendly atmosphere.

Liquid Planet, 11002 Clifton Blvd., will blend the bejesus out of wheatgrass and spirulina for you. It also has rice bowls, wraps and other healthy-ish fast food. A Thai restaurant, Asian Grille, is at 11100 Clifton Blvd. Informal Mexican food arrives on very hot plates at El Jalapeno, 1313 W. 117th St., though you can find much better Mexican and Latin fare a few miles south in Westown (see p. 189).

Edgewater also happens to be Cleveland's epicenter of 24-hour diners. The two most popular are My Friends, 11616 Detroit Ave., where after-hours wreckage begins to wash up around 2 a.m.; and Dianna's Deli and Restaurant, 1332 W. 117th St. (technically in Lakewood).

Opportunities for caffeination are plentiful. MoCa (short for "More than Caffeine" – they serve sandwiches too), 10435 Clifton Ave., opened in 2011. Truffles, 11122 Clifton Blvd., seems forever to be cycling in and out of business. At the time of printing it was closed, but a new incarnation will likely emerge soon. It has a loyal gay clientele and serves pastries. Starbucks also has a comfy location at 11501 Clifton Ave.

On the bar scene, The Clifton Martini and Wine Bar, 10427 Clifton Ave., is a dignified newcomer to the neighborhood; it has an outdoor patio. Drawing a more blue-collar clientele is Johnny Malloy's Sports Pub, 11636 Clifton Ave.

Two bars in the neighborhood offer live music. Brothers Lounge, 11609 Detroit Ave., has mostly jazz and blues in a nice renovated space. Now That's Class, 11213 Detroit Ave., is a punk bar offering concerts, vegan food and free beer on Thursday nights if you ride your bike.

For gay men, there's the already-mentioned Twist, 11633 Clifton Blvd., probably Cleveland's cleanest-cut gay bar. The crowd skews toward 30- and 40-something professionals, though younger and older folks come too.

An old-school gay leather bar, The Hawk, is at 11217 Detroit Ave. The provocatively named Bottoms Up, 1572 W. 117th St. in Lakewood, draws a mixed-race crowd of gay men and women and has drag shows on weekends. Cocktails, 9208 Detroit Ave., in a bleak patch of city between Detroit Shoreway and Edgewater, has a surprisingly cozy interior. On Sunday and Wednesday nights, it offers the best karaoke in town; the selection of songs is huge and the crowd mixed and fun.

Edgewater: The Once Over

Edgewater isn't really a destination neighborhood, so you can come anytime and get an authentic look at what it's like to live here.

Start your tour at W. 110th St. and Clifton Boulevard. Here you'll see Liquid Planet, Pet-Tique and (nearby) the Clifton Avenue Wine Bar. Walk west on Clifton, away from Downtown – the addresses should be getting higher. You'll pass some typical apartment buildings and houses; note phone numbers if you're interested. Also along the way will be Truffles, Anytime Fitness, Flower Child and Big Fun.

Once you hit W. 117th Street – the border between Lakewood and Cleveland – double back. At W. 116th St., turn right (South). You'll encounter more typical housing and cross some railroad tracks before ascending a little hill to Detroit Avenue. At the intersection with Detroit, you'll see stores like Bent Crayon, Chelsea's, and My Friend's. Turn left on Detroit and head East for a few blocks, taking in this part of the neighborhood.

At W. 110th Street, turn left, returning to Clifton Boulevard where you started. If you'd like to see some of the neighborhood's more upscale housing, keep going North on W. 110th. First you'll cross Lake Avenue, which has some nice apartment buildings (again, take down numbers if you like!) and then Edgewater Drive. Turn right on Edgewater and walk west (toward Downtown) as long as time permits. If you get as far as West Boulevard, you'll see the entrance to Edgewater State Park.

Double back and return to Clifton and W. 110th, unwinding at whichever restaurant, bar or coffee shop looked most appealing during your walk.

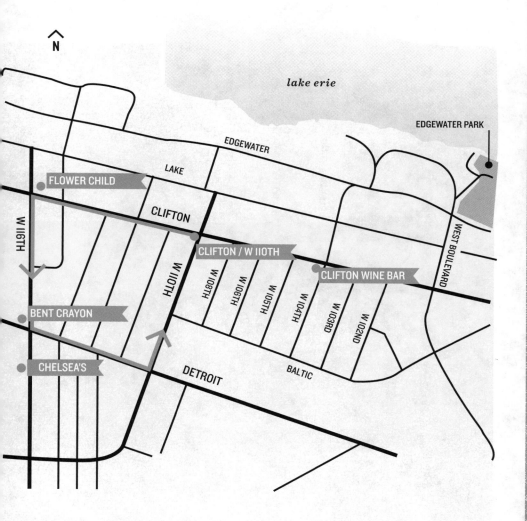

lake erie

EDGEWATER PARK

EDGEWATER

LAKE

FLOWER CHILD

CLIFTON

CLIFTON / W 110TH

CLIFTON WINE BAR

W 116TH

W 110TH

W 108TH

W 106TH

W 105TH

W 104TH

W 103RD

W 102ND

WEST BOULEVARD

BENT CRAYON

CHELSEA'S

DETROIT

BALTIC

Deweys Coffee on Shaker Square

day 11/100

SHAKER SQUARE, BUCKEYE, & LARCHMERE

SHAKER SQUARE, BUCKEYE, AND LARCHMERE

———

Shaker Square is on the eastern edge of the City of Cleveland. Centered around the Shaker Square Rapid Station, and with plenty of apartment buildings dating from the 1920s and 1930s, it's one of the densest neighborhoods in the city.

The neighborhood came into being in the 1920s on land owned by the Van Sweringen brothers, private developers who also built Terminal Tower. In the days before automobile dominance, the Van Sweringens needed to provide a fast connection to Downtown in order to attract residents. Their solution was to buy an old rail right-of-way connecting their land to Terminal Tower – and the Shaker Rapid was born.

The Square itself is actually a circle, with the Rapid running through the middle to both Downtown and points East and Southeast. Around the circle are stores and restaurants, while the side streets contain apartment buildings and some houses. The apartment buildings are some of the stateliest in Cleveland, particularly those along North and South Moreland boulevards, and along Drexmore Road.

About a block north of the Square is Larchmere Boulevard, a quiet commercial street with more restaurants and shops. Buckeye Road, meanwhile, is a busy artery lying about two blocks south of the Square; it has a mix of old storefronts and new shopping plazas.

Shaker Square itself is a fairly well-integrated place. On a typical weekend night you'll find a mix of black, white and Asian people from the neighborhood sharing sidewalks with well-heeled visitors from the suburbs. Yet, as elsewhere in Cleveland, there are distinct racial

12,470
{ population }

73/100
Shaker/Buckeye's
Walk Score

LOCATION

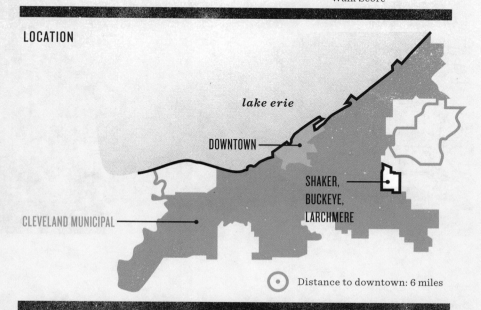

lake erie

DOWNTOWN

SHAKER,
BUCKEYE,
LARCHMERE

CLEVELAND MUNICIPAL

Distance to downtown: 6 miles

WHO SHOULD LIVE HERE?

Student

Families

Professional

Empty nester

Artist

No car needed

AMENITIES AND COMMUNITY FEATURES:

Rapid Transit	Museums	Park	Specialty Shops
Grocery Stores	Retail Shopping	Yoga	Concert Hall
Restaurants	Bookstore	Bars/Nightlife	Pharmacy
Movie Theaters	Gym	Community Garden	Farmers Market
Library	Coffee Shop	Live Theater	Sports

divides among residential areas. White and Asian people tend to live North and East of the Square, while blacks live South and West.

The neighborhood tends to skew to both extremes of the age spectrum. Many residents have been here for years, settled into apartment buildings or houses and attracted to the simultaneously walkable and quiet streets. Patrons at many of the restaurants sport white hair and blazers. But a lot of 20-something students and medical residents live here, too, because of the neighborhood's proximity to University Circle, a mile or two away. Because the former population is settled, and the latter transient, you won't find the same sense of change and evolution as in closer-in neighborhoods like Ohio City and Tremont – but the more established air will be just what some people are seeking.

A quirk of this neighborhood is that, on some blocks, you can live in the City of Cleveland but send your children to Shaker Heights public schools. In general, these blocks lie East

The Belgian Village day 6/100

and Southeast of Shaker Square, butting right up to the Cleveland border. Realty listings will tell you which school district a given house is in.

Transportation
The neighborhood grew up around a Rapid station, so it's one of the most transit-friendly places in Cleveland. A ride from Shaker Square to Downtown takes about 12 minutes, and trains run every 15 minutes or so (more frequently during rush hour).

Two lines – Blue and Green – run through Shaker Square. They run together from Downtown to the Square, at which point they diverge. The Green Line goes East along Shaker Boulevard to Green Road in eastern Shaker Heights. The Blue Line goes Southeast along Van Aken Boulevard to the busy intersection of Warrensville Center Road. The lines traverse mostly quiet residential areas, so if you live in Shaker Square you're unlikely to use the Rapid for anything but going back and forth to Downtown.

The only transit connection to University Circle is the #48 bus, which takes about 15 minutes to snake its way downhill to University Hospitals and Severance Hall.

Because of the Rapid to Downtown and the range of amenities in the neighborhood, Shaker Square is one of the best places in Cleveland to live car-free or car-light. There's even a City Wheels car stationed next to the Shaker Square Rapid Station. You can rent by the hour when you need your own wheels. (For more information, see box p. 207 – Living in Cleveland Without a Car.)

Shaker Square sits on the same plateau above Downtown as does Cleveland Heights. Roadway connections downhill are few and tend to be traffic-choked, so it's not very pleasant walking or riding a bicycle between Shaker Square and either Downtown or University Circle. From the Square, the main route down to University Circle is twisty Martin Luther King Jr. Boulevard; on the way back you'll be coming up Stokes Boulevard. Both are one-way and jammed with speeding cars at rush hours. The good news is that once you're in University Circle, you can pick up dedicated bicycle lanes on Euclid Avenue to get Downtown.

There's an effort underway to build a dedicated bike path from Shaker Heights and Shaker Square to University Circle, and from there north to Lake Erie. But a lack of funding has made the timeline for the path's completion uncertain.

As on much of the East Side, freeways are distant. The closest is either I-90 at MLK, or I-490 (which connects to I-77 and I-71) at E. 55th Street. Both are some four miles away, and to reach I-490 you'll go through some of the most sobering urban abandonment in the nation.

Housing
Dozens of pretty apartment buildings line North Moreland, South Moreland, Shaker and Drexmore boulevards. Many date from the 1920s and 1930s and – while they boast the great woodwork and architectural details of that era – have seen better days. I lived in an apartment on North Moreland where the kitchen ceiling caved in from water damage.

Because of student turnover, there are usually units available in just about every building. Late spring and early summer are the best times to look, before the influx of Case Western students returns. One of the biggest (if not best-reviewed) landlords is Montlack Realty, 2590 North Moreland Blvd. Their nicest building may be the art-deco Cormere, 2661 North

Moreland Blvd. But the best way to find openings is to walk around, spotting "For Rent" signs. You can also check Larchmere and Buckeye roads for apartments above storefronts. Rents range between $500 and $700 for studios and one-bedrooms, and $800 and up for two-bedrooms in good condition. Heat is almost always included.

You can buy condos in the regal Moreland Court apartment buildings, built in the 1920s on Shaker Boulevard between Shaker Square and Coventry Road. These offer some of the best condo deals in town, with units starting at around $50,000 — but beware condo fees. (Visit www.morelandcourts.org.) The buildings are home to musicians in The Cleveland Orchestra, professors and other local intelligentsia.

More typical Cleveland-style housing can be found on the numbered side streets off of Larchmere, Buckeye, Fairhill and MLK. You can find apartments on these streets, too, mostly in two-family houses. These will go for less than in the bigger apartment buildings nearby, but be aware that you'll be paying your own heating bill in most of these places.

If you're looking to buy, you can find single-families and doubles off of both Larchmere and Buckeye. These are very affordable, but the further West you go the sketchier the neighborhood. The most affluent pocket of houses is the clutch of streets (Cormere, Ardoon, Haddam) between Larchmere and Shaker Boulevard, east of Shaker Square. Here you'll find early 20th century homes in good repair; this part of the neighborhood is in the Shaker Heights school district.

Groceries & Shopping

The Shaker Square Farmers' Market – the largest in the city – is fast becoming the neighborhood's calling card. Farmers come here from all over Northeast Ohio to sell their wares, and customers have followed, snapping up a bounty of local vegetables, fruit, meat, honey, grain and dairy. The diversity of goods is a thrilling testament to Ohio's agricultural might. In the summer months you can buy just about any kind of food you need here; in winter, the market gets smaller and goes indoors, selling mostly dry goods and cold-storage produce. Beyond the food itself, the market offers great people watching. The market runs on Saturdays from 8 a.m. to noon.

Dave's Supermarket, 13130 Shaker Square, is walking distance to most parts of the neighborhood. Like the local chain's other stores, it's not fancy, but is more than adequate

for daily needs. Further south, there's a Giant Eagle in the shopping plaza at 11501 Buckeye Rd. Larchmere Deli & Beverage, 12727 Larchmere Blvd., has beer, wine and chips.

Many of the retail spaces on the Square itself are now occupied by restaurants. Probably the most interesting non-food establishment is Play Matters, 13214 Shaker Square, an independent toy shop. Also here are a CVS Pharmacy, 13215 Shaker Square, and Lake Erie Artists, which sells crafts and gifts by local artisans, 13129 Shaker Square.

Larchmere offers more to interest the casual shopper. There's Loganberry Books, 13015 Larchmere Blvd., which bursts with new and used books and where you can while away hours on a cozy overstuffed chair. The store also offers bookbinding lessons; contact the store for more information. Nearby are Fine Points Yarn Shop, 12620 Larchmere Blvd.; The Dancing Sheep (gifts), 12712 Larchmere Blvd.; and Frog's Legs (men's clothing), 12807

Larchmere Blvd. You can find a bevy of antique stores here, too. Try Marc Goodman's Antique Mall, 12721 Larchmere Blvd., or Conservation Studios, 12702 Larchmere Blvd. A good time to sample all the street's offerings is the annual Holiday Stroll on Thanksgiving weekend.

Health & Recreation

From Shaker Square, it's about a mile and a half to Shaker Lakes, a linear park that follows Doan Brook through Shaker Heights and Cleveland Heights. Here you'll find miles of jogging and bicycle trails and picnic areas. The Nature Center at Shaker Lakes, 2600 South Park Blvd. in Shaker Heights, has nature programs and an interpretive trail through a marsh.

There's no traditional gym in the neighborhood; for that you'll have to travel to Bally's in Cleveland Heights or 1-2-1 Fitness Center in University Circle. But there's a personal training studio, Beyond Fitness, at 13005 Larchmere Blvd. Cleveland City Dance, 13110 Shaker Square, offers dance and yoga classes for kids and adults. The Passport Project, an arts and community center at 12801 Buckeye Rd., also has dance lessons, along with capoeira instruction.

South of Shaker Square, in the Kinsman neighborhood, is the not-so-secret Schvitz, at E. 116th Street and Luke Avenue just north of Kinsman Road, perhaps the only remaining holdover from the neighborhood's Jewish days. The place attracts businessmen who walk around in towels, eat steak and smoke cigars.

Eating & Drinking Out

There's no shortage of places to eat out. Venerable Hungarian restaurant Balaton, 13133 Shaker Square, anchors the northwest quadrant of the Square; here you'll find stroganoff and spaetzle and other yummy if bloating delights. (The area around Buckeye Road was a predominantly Hungarian neighborhood until about the 1970s.)

Also on the Square itself is fire food and drink (yes, that's all lower-case, thank you), 13220 Shaker Square, with some of Cleveland's most creative contemporary cuisine; Sasa Matsu, 13120 Shaker Square, with excellent sushi; and Sarava, 13225 Shaker Square, with Brazilian food. (Sarava has the same owner as Sergio's in University Circle.) Zanzibar Soul Fusion, 13114 Shaker Square, serves soul food, while Grotto Wine Bar, 13101 Shaker Square, serves Italian dishes and doubles as a wine bar.

For no-frills diner food in a family atmosphere, settle into Yours Truly, 13228 Shaker Square.

Up on Larchmere, you'll find a couple of old-school places popular with the white-hair set. Academy Tavern, 12800 Larchmere Blvd., is a straight-ahead pub with grub, while the Larchmere Tavern, 13051 Larchmere Blvd., dishes conservative plates for conservative palates. But the street also has some more contemporary dining spots. Maybe the brightest star is Felice Urban Café, 12502 Larchmere Blvd., with food by the same guy who cooks at Fat Cats in Tremont. Flying Cranes Café, 13006 Larchmere Blvd., cooks delicious Japanese cuisine. Menu 6, 12718 Larchmere Blvd., offers contemporary American cuisine, while the beloved Big Al's Diner, 12600 Larchmere Blvd., has gut-busting breakfasts and lunches.

True to the neighborhood's sedate ambience, there aren't really any bars per se; most of your drinking will be done at bars inside restaurants. The lovely patio of Sarava, where you can order Brazilian drinks like the caiparinha while looking out on the Square, deserves special mention; Grotto, as mentioned, doubles as a wine bar.

The neighborhood coffee shops are Deweys Coffee House, 13201 Shaker Square, with fair-trade coffee and homemade caramel corn; and Urbean Joe Gourmet Coffee, 12404 Larchmere Blvd.

Shaker Square: The Once Over

If you can, come on a Saturday morning. There will be a lot of non-residents in the Square for the farmers' market, but the market is one of the neighborhood's biggest assets and you should get a taste of what it's like if you're thinking of living here.

Start on the Square itself. There's parking on North and South Moreland boulevards, as well as behind the CVS Pharmacy (enter the lot via Cormere Street). If you're here during market hours in the summer, the farmers will be set up in the middle of the Square; check out what's on offer. In the winter, the market moves to an empty storefront next to Deweys Coffee.

Take a stroll around the Square, noting the restaurants and shops and the Dave's Supermarket. Also see the Rapid station at the western edge of the Square. At South

Shaker Square Farmers Market

day 1/100

Moreland, you can walk a few blocks South to see some nice if shop-worn apartment buildings; note any numbers. If you go far enough, you'll come to Buckeye Road, where you can visit The Passport Project at 12801 Buckeye Rd.

Double back and return to the Square, and head North on North Moreland. More apartment buildings are here. Note any phone numbers of interest. In a block you'll come to Larchmere Boulevard; turn left, toward Downtown.

Between North Moreland and about E. 121st Street, you'll find a cozy commercial district with lots of shops to explore; see above for listings. If you're hungry, you can stop for a light bite to eat at Flying Cranes.

The side streets south of Larchmere – particularly those between E. 130th and E. 126th streets – have pleasant rows of single- and two-family houses. These are home to a mix of people from various economic and racial backgrounds. There's also a pocket of very nice homes north of Lachmere, around E. 126th Street. See in particular Britton Drive.

Double back on Larchmere and head East past North Moreland Boulevard. On this part of Larchmere you'll see a grand tree canopy and some gorgeous homes; the north side of the block is Shaker Heights, while the south side is Cleveland. The streets south of Larchmere (Haddam, Ardoon, Cormere) have middle class homes where you can live in the City of Cleveland but send your kids to Shaker schools.

At Coventry Road, If you have time, you can keep walking east on Larchmere for three blocks to reach Shaker Lakes park. (Larchmere splits off into South Park Boulevard, North Woodland Road and West Park Boulevard, any of which will take you into the park.)

After checking out the park, head South on Coventry for a block until you reach Shaker Boulevard. Here you'll see another Rapid station – this one a stop for the Green Line. If you have time, you can turn left and keep walking East into Shaker Heights, taking in some of the suburb's stately mansions. Otherwise turn right on Shaker Boulevard, back toward Downtown. On both sides of the street you'll see the stately Moreland Courts buildings. These are condos, but the owners will sometimes rent their units; check places like Craig's List for availability.

Once you come back to Shaker Square, you can take a load off at any of the restaurants or at Dewey's Coffee House.

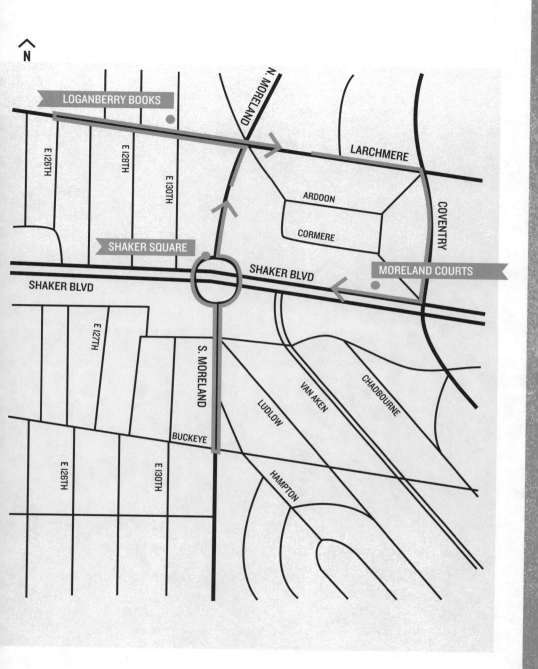

N

LOGANBERRY BOOKS

E 126TH

E 128TH

E 130TH

N. MORELAND

LARCHMERE

ARDOON

CORMERE

COVENTRY

SHAKER SQUARE

SHAKER BLVD

MORELAND COURTS

SHAKER BLVD

E 127TH

S. MORELAND

VAN AKEN

CHADBOURNE

LUDLOW

BUCKEYE

E 126TH

E 130TH

HAMPTON

— NORTH —
COLLINWOOD

Live performance at the Beachland Tavern

day 10/100

NORTH COLLINWOOD

In many ways North Collinwood, about nine miles east of Downtown, mirrors Detroit Shoreway to the West. Both neighborhoods have working class histories, easy access to Lake Erie, and are home to a racially diverse population of professionals, artists and long-time working class residents. Both have old Eastern European churches and meat shops. Even the architecture is similar: densely packed brick storefronts and solid, century-old housing.

But while Detroit Shoreway is betting on live theater and movies to lead its revitalization, North Collinwood has embraced music and the visual arts. The Beachland Ballroom, 15711 Waterloo Rd., anchors this emerging scene. Run by long-time local music booker Cindy Barber, the music club draws local and national acts, with specialties in indie rock (think Arcade Fire before they were huge) and roots/Americana. It's a former Croatian ballroom, so while you listen to great music you can gaze at colorful wall paintings of old-country musicians and peasants.

The neighborhood, like so many in Cleveland, traces its roots to Eastern Europe. It boomed in the 1910s and 1920s as immigrants from Slovenia, Croatia and Poland settled here to work in the nearby rail yards. Many of these families have since migrated East, to places like Willoughby and Mentor, but a few of their old stores remain, including the well-regarded meat shops R&D Sausage Co., 15714 Waterloo Rd., and Raddell's Sausage Shop, 478 E. 152nd St. The neighborhood has become increasingly diverse since the 1970s and 1980s.

16,761
{ population }

62/100
North Collinwood's
Walk Score

LOCATION

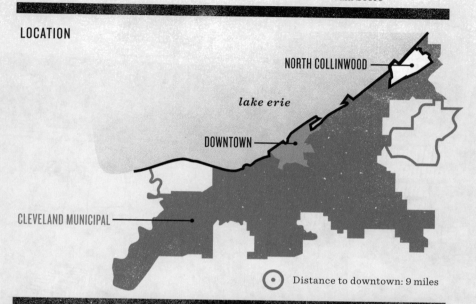

NORTH COLLINWOOD

lake erie

DOWNTOWN

CLEVELAND MUNICIPAL

Distance to downtown: 9 miles

WHO SHOULD LIVE HERE?

Student

Families

Professional

Empty nester

Artist

AMENITIES AND COMMUNITY FEATURES:

Rapid Transit	Museums	Park	Specialty Shops
Grocery Stores	Retail Shopping	Yoga	Concert Hall
Restaurants	Bookstore	Bars/Nightlife	Pharmacy
Movie Theaters	Gym	Community Garden	Farmers Market
Library	Coffee Shop	Live Theater	Sports

Music Saves

day 91/100

A wave of new interest in North Collinwood began with the Beachland's opening in 2001. Adjacent to it on Waterloo Road have sprouted junk stores, record shops and a coffee house. Another main commercial artery, E. 185th Street, on the border with the suburb of Euclid, has been more stable. It offers a full slate of service retail and restaurants, along with a drab but useful assortment of laundromats and accounting offices. (See below for specific listings for both districts.)

The side streets surrounding these commercial districts can be roughshod – and even Waterloo Road itself hasn't completely shaken off the doldrums of past decline. But many houses are coming back to life thanks to transplants from the suburbs and from bigger, more expensive cities.

North Collinwood is a lakefront neighborhood, and the blocks closest to Lake Erie look like they snuck in from a well-heeled suburb. Many of the streets north of Lakeshore Boulevard dead end at the lakefront, and the residents enjoy private beach access. Some artists live here, but there's also a longstanding population of upper- and middle-class residents. City of Cleveland employees, who until recently were required by law to live in the city proper, own some of these houses.

North Collinwood's boundaries are Lake Erie and I-90 to the North and South, respectively; and E. 140th Street and E. 185th Street to the West and East.

Transportation

Unlike most other East Side neighborhoods, North Collinwood has excellent freeway access. I-90 runs along its southern border, with the E. 152nd – E. 156th Street exit just a few blocks from Waterloo Road. I-90 will get you Downtown in under 10 minutes when traffic is light. You can drive to University Circle and Cleveland Heights in about 15 minutes.

Without a car, though, the neighborhood can feel isolated – a function of its distance from Downtown. There's no Rapid station, and a bus trip to the city center can take close to an hour.

If you're an intrepid cyclist, you can get Downtown via Lakeshore Boulevard through Bratenahl – a posh suburb carved out of the city just to the West of North Collinwood – and then to the Cleveland Lakefront Bikeway. The bikeway isn't as official as it sounds.

It's a hodge-podge of city streets, some actual bike path around Gordon Park, and a barely used freeway marginal going into Downtown. Still, it's a direct route to the city center and has some nice views of Lake Erie along the way.

Housing

North Collinwood covers a large area, and its housing ranges from early 20th century doubles and single-families to post-war bungalows and apartment towers. Newer housing, unsurprisingly, clusters around the eastern border of the neighborhood near the suburb of Euclid.

The area around Waterloo Road offers prototypical Cleveland doubles and wood-frame single family houses, mixed with four- and eight-unit apartment buildings. Sales prices and rents are some of the most affordable in town.

From east of E. 146th Street, you'll find a succession of private "beach club" streets branching north off Lakeshore Boulevard toward Lake Erie. A private beach caps each of these streets. Houses on these blocks are closely packed, well-built and well-maintained, but even here prices are quite affordable – particularly in the wake of the mortgage crisis. Former U.S. Senator, Ohio Governor and Cleveland Mayor George Voinovich lives on one of these streets.

Post-war apartment buildings, including some high rises with lake views, line Lakeshore Boulevard. Most of these have seen better days.

Groceries & Shopping

Dave's Supermarket, 15900 Lakeshore Blvd., is the neighborhood's largest supermarket. It's fairly no-frills, but will have most of what you need. It lies about three-quarters of a mile north of the Waterloo district. Save a Lot operates a branch at 18501 Neff Rd.

The Coit Road Farmers Market lies about 2 miles south of North Collinwood in the struggling suburb of East Cleveland (15000 Woodworth Road). It's one of the region's best and oldest markets, open Saturday mornings all year round and on Wednesday mornings from April to November.

Waterloo Road has seen a handful of interesting stores open in recent years. One of the earliest pioneers among them was Music Saves, 15801 Waterloo Rd., an independent record shop that stays open late to catch customers from shows at the Beachland

Ballroom. This Way Out, a thrift store in the basement of the Beachland Ballroom, 15711 Waterloo Rd., is open during shows and has a tasteful selection of men's and women's clothing.

C9 Boutique, 15613 Waterloo Rd., peddles vintage clothes and some new threads (men's and women's) by local designers. The Head Shop, 15615 Waterloo Rd., is – well, a head shop, full of bongs and Bob Marley regalia.

Native Cleveland, 15813 Waterloo Rd., has well-designed, Cleveland-themed T-shirts and other gifts. Right next door, Star Pop bursts at the seams with owner Troy Schwartz's impressive vintage and junk collection, including thousands of old T-shirts. He does a lot of his business online, but the retail location is worth a visit for its sheer eccentricity and the trove of Cleveland memorabilia from the 1970s, 1960s and earlier. Another vintage store – clothes, records, etc. – is Blue Arrow Records & Boutique, 16001 Waterloo Rd., Its floor is paved in laminated LP covers.

Several more old-school shops offer repair services. Azure Stained Glass, 15602 Waterloo Rd., focuses on leaded glass window repairs and opens only by appointment. Tony's Furniture Refinishing and Upholstery, 15303 Waterloo Rd., will polish up all the old swag you find in the vintage stores up the street.

E. 185th Street, on the border with the suburb of Euclid, has gathered some dust over the years and has a decidedly less "hipster" feel than Waterloo. But you'll still find tons on offer here. Some of the more interesting shops include (moving roughly from North to South): Blue Sky Bicycles, 565 E. 185th St.; Tuthill's Flowers, 557 E. 185th St.; Resurrection Cycle Motorcycle Shop, 627 E. 185th St.; Music Emporium, selling musical instruments, 670 E. 185th St.; Promises Bridal and Formal Wear, 632 E. 185th St.; Martin's Men's Wear, 696 E. 185th St.; King Gallery, with furniture and African art, 700 E. 185th St.; and Shore Carpet, 854 E. 185th St.

For pharmacy and toiletries you can hit either Rite Aid, 475 E. 185th St., or Walgreen's, 15609 Lakeshore Blvd. There's a post office branch at 891 E. 185th St.

Richmond Town Square, 691 Richmond Rd. in the neighboring suburb of Richmond Heights, offers a Macy's, JCPenney and Sears, plus a large cinema.

Health & Recreation

Lake Erie is the star natural attraction of North Collinwood. Three state parks, crammed between E. 156th Street and Neff Road north of Lakeshore Boulevard, provide public access to the lakefront. One, Euclid Beach, was once home to a large amusement park; today, the only relic is the former entrance gate. The beach is marred by some high-rise apartment buildings dating from the 1970s. Wildwood and Villa Angela parks have a more natural feel, with beaches. You can also reach Gordon Park and Rockefeller Park in University Circle via the Cleveland Lakefront Bikeway.

At 16500 Lakeshore Blvd., the City of Cleveland has renovated an old Big Lots discount store into a new public recreation center – one of the largest and nicest in town. The Collinwood Recreation Center opened in Fall 2011 and achieved LEED certification for its green building practices. It's home to an indoor track, a gymnasium and class spaces.

Nu Life Fitness Camp, 15430 Waterloo Rd., offers boot camp-style fitness classes.

A few miles southeast of North Collinwood, in the neighboring suburbs of Euclid and Richmond Heights, the Cleveland MetroParks maintains the Euclid Creek Reservation. It's not one of the park system's star green spaces, but it has pleasant biking and walking trails.

For medical care, the campus of Euclid Hospital (part of the Cleveland Clinic system), sprawls across several acres on E. 185th Street north of Lakeshore. There's also a veterinary clinic, Love'n Care Animal Hospital, at 820 E. 185th St.

Eating & Dining Out

Options for dining out in North Collinwood aren't as numerous as in other city neighborhoods, but what's here is pretty special.

Tucked away on a residential block north of Waterloo Road is the Grovewood Tavern, 17105 Grovewood Ave. This is one of the city's coziest restaurants, serving upscale comfort food in a well-worn interior. Arts Collinwood Café, 15605 Waterloo Rd., daylights as a coffee shop and then turns into a bustling, European-style café at night. Bratenahl Kitchen West Indies Cuisine, 14002 Lakeshore Blvd., offers American cooking with an "Island flare."

For a taste of Old Cleveland, head to the Slovenian Workmen's Home, 15335 Waterloo Rd., an 85-year-old social hall that you can visit for a Friday fish fry or a Sunday polka dance.

Over on E. 185th Street, the best-known place is probably Bistro 185, 991 E. 185th St. Here you'll find tasty new American dishes in an upscale but non-fussy setting. Lovers of lasagna and eggplant parmesan swear by Scotti's Italian Eatery, 882 E. 185th St.

Delicious, greasy pizza comes out of the ovens at Villa Rosa, 853 E. 185th St. Meanwhile, Chili Peppers, 869 E. 185th St., puts a local twist on the Chipotle-style burrito formula. The street also boasts a pair of greasy spoon diners: Lucky Restaurant, 742 E. 185th St., and Gus's Diner, 797 E. 185th St.

Hidden in a nondescript building at 14906 Lakeshore Blvd. is Archie's Lake Shore Bakery. Archie keeps alive the tradition of Hough Bakery, a now-defunct local chain of bakeries famous for its sugary cakes. (Archie himself is a former Hough employee.) You can order cakes for birthdays and other special occasions by calling 216-481-4188.

Several old-fashioned pubs line E. 185th Street, including Cebar's Euclid Tavern, 595 E. 185th St.; Harland Pub, 779 E. 185th St.; and the popular Muldoon's Saloon and Eatery, 1020 E. 185th St. Of a similar ilk is Mark's Time-Out Grille, 17910 Lakeshore Blvd.

North Collinwood: The Once Over

It's tough (though certainly not impossible) to get a full picture of North Collinwood on a single walk. The neighborhood is divided into two distinct districts (Waterloo and E. 185th Street) that lie about a mile and a half apart. The easiest thing to do is walk the Waterloo Road district first, and then do a driving tour of the area around E. 185th Street.

Waterloo is most active at night, when there are shows at the Beachland Ballroom; at other times it's downright sleepy. If you'd like to see the neighborhood at its busiest, come after 7 p.m. Park near the Beachland, 15711 Waterloo Rd. Parking right on Waterloo can be challenging, but there are usually spaces on Trafalgar Avenue, which is the street that runs parallel to Waterloo behind the club.

If the Beachland is open, you can check out the concert calendar and head downstairs to the This Way Out vintage store. Then walk East down Waterloo Road, with Downtown to your back. You'll pass stores like Native Cleveland and Star Pop and the great Music Saves. Farther down is Blue Arrow Records & Boutique, recognizable by the – you guessed it – giant blue arrow out front.

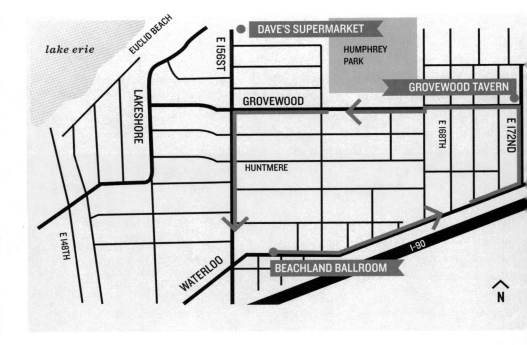

Keep walking on Waterloo until you come to E. 172nd Street. Turn left. The next cross street is Grovewood, and you'll see the Grovewood Tavern & Wine Bar. Turn left on Grovewood, taking in some typical Collinwood housing. You'll pass Humphrey Park, a plain if serviceable green space maintained by the City, on your right.

At E. 156th Street, turn left. In a few blocks you'll return to Waterloo. Make a right on Waterloo and walk until you come to E. 152nd St. You'll pass a few more independent shops. At the triangular intersection you'll see the Arts Collinwood Café. You can stop in here to recap your tour. The large Waterloo Tower outside the café, designed by artist Christopher Diehl, was unveiled in 2010. (Across the street is Raddell's Sausage Shop, one of the holdouts from the "old" neighborhood.)

Next, get back in your car and drive North on E. 156th Street, retracing the route you just took on foot. In about 10 blocks you'll come to the bleak – if useful – intersection of E. 156th Street and Lakeshore Boulevard. Dave's Supermarket is here, along with a Walgreen's and the entrance to Euclid Beach State Park.

Turn right (East) on Lakeshore Boulevard. Over the next few blocks the landscape becomes greener, and you'll come to the entrance for Wildwood State Park. If you have time, drive through the park. Also here is the Memorial-Nottingham branch of the Cleveland Public Library, 17133 Lakeshore Blvd.

Keep going on Lakeshore. To get a sense of lakeside living in North Collinwood, you could explore any of the blocks north of Lakeshore, including Ingleside Road and Rosecliff Road.

At E. 185th Street – the border with the suburb of Euclid – turn right (South), away from the Lake. As you head South, you'll pass through a still-vital commercial artery with tons of convenience and service retail. (See above for listings.)

On the blocks of E. 185th closest to the interchange with I-90, you'll pass the well-regarded Bistro 185 and the unassuming Muldoon's Saloon & Eatery. You can either merge onto the freeway or continue South on E. 185th. The street changes names a few times before turning into Highland Road and passing through the Euclid Creek Reservation of the Cleveland MetroParks and into the suburb of Richmond Heights.

Cleveland Beaches

day 56/100

WEST PARK

Kayaking

day 92/100

WEST PARK

"West Park" is the collective name for the comfortable, working- and middle-class neighborhoods of Cleveland's far West Side. Reflective of its strong Irish Catholic heritage, the area is organized more by parish than by traditional geographic boundaries.

West Park lies in a kind of panhandle of the city south of Lakewood. To the West is the Rocky River valley (also the western boundary of the city) and to the South lies the airport. The eastern boundary is Puritas Avenue. Lorain Avenue is the main east-west artery. The area east of Puritas to W. 117th St. is known as Westown, though in some ways Westown and West Park operate as a single unit. (See p. 189)

Until 2010, employees of the City of Cleveland were required to live in the city proper. West Park has been an especially popular address among firefighters and police officers with children who might otherwise have chosen the suburbs. The neighborhood for years billed itself as "the suburb in the City," and that's a fairly accurate description. It's not entirely suburban – you can still walk places, and access to the Rapid is some of the best in town. But the neighborhood's ball fields, leafy side streets and neat lawns give West Park a "Leave It to Beaver" atmosphere you won't find in most urban places.

Given that cultural reference, you won't be surprised to learn there's little that is hip or trendy about West Park. Most of what's here has been here for decades. For many people, that will be an attractor, but those looking for a more creative, edgy vibe will be best advised to set their sights elsewhere.

55,367
{ population }

59/100
West Park's Walk Score

LOCATION

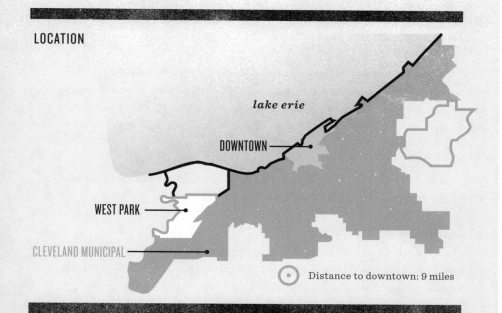

lake erie

DOWNTOWN →

WEST PARK →

CLEVELAND MUNICIPAL →

⊙ Distance to downtown: 9 miles

WHO SHOULD LIVE HERE?

Student

Families

Professional

Empty nester

AMENITIES AND COMMUNITY FEATURES:

Rapid Transit	Museums	Park	Specialty Shops
Grocery Stores	Retail Shopping	Yoga	Concert Hall
Restaurants	Bookstore	Bars/Nightlife	Pharmacy
Movie Theaters	Gym	Community Garden	Farmers Market
Library	Coffee Shop	Live Theater	Sports

The neighborhood boomed from the 1920s through the 1960s, as families (mostly Irish) made their way West from closer-in neighborhoods like Ohio City. While Irish identity is still strong, recent years have seen the arrival of Middle Eastern, Latino and African American households. There are mosques and a Zen temple, Cloudwater Zendo, 14436 Puritas Ave. Beth Israel, the last synagogue in the City proper and the only one in the region West of the Cuyahoga River, is at 14308 Triskett Rd. (In 2010, the synagogue announced plans to move to the suburb of North Olmsted, but still needs to raise millions of dollars for a new building.)

Riverside Elementary School is regarded as one of the best in the city. But many families who have the financial means send their kids to one of several Catholic schools in the neighborhood. These are feeder schools for St. Ignatius High School in Ohio City and St. Edward's in Lakewood (boys) and St. Joe's in West Park or Magnificat High School in Rocky River (girls).

Since the neighborhood is so close to the airport, noise from planes can be a problem. The farther north and east you are, the quieter the engines will be.

Transportation

West Park has two stops on the Rapid's Red Line: West Park Station and Puritas Station. Both are primarily park-and-rides, surrounded by dispiriting expanses of asphalt. Puritas has the more attractive pedestrian entrance, around W. 157th Street and Valleyview; there's really no pleasant way to walk to the West Park station. From either station, it's about five minutes to the airport and 15 to 20 minutes to Downtown. Buses are likely to be slow given the distance to Downtown (about eight to 10 miles).

Lots of stores and amenities concentrate around the intersection of Rocky River Drive and Lorain Avenue – known as Kamm's Corners. If you want to be able to walk places, you're best off living within a half mile of here, either north or south of Lorain.

Bicycling isn't hugely prevalent in this neighborhood, though some people cycle to the Rapid stations to go Downtown. There's a bicycle shop, Lorain Triskett Cycle and Fitness, at 15718 Lorain Ave.

You can access just about all of Cleveland's freeways from West Park. I-90 has exits at W. 140th St. and McKinley Avenue; you can reach I-71 from W. 150th Street or from near the airport. Either will get you Downtown in 10 minutes when there's no traffic. You can also reach I-480 (and, from it, I-77) around the airport.

Housing

West Park was one of the last-developed neighborhoods in Cleveland. As a result, you'll find post-World War II bungalows and Cape Cods mixed in with more traditional Cleveland Colonials from the 1920s and 1930s.

Well-kept blocks abound, but some of the nicest are west of Warren Road around Edgecliff Avenue, where some streets are still paved in brick. From these blocks, you could also walk to the Giant Eagle grocery store at Warren Village.

Also attractive are the blocks off of Rocky River Drive, north and south of Lorain. You'll find many fine brick Cape Cods and bungalows here. The blocks west of Rocky River Drive (e.g. Greenwood and Ernadale) dead end at the steep Rocky River Valley. These are probably the most desirable in the neighborhood, and have a strong concentration of young families with children. Rocky River Drive becomes increasingly dreary as you go south toward the airport, but the side streets are well-kept.

There are also some apartment buildings (mostly postwar) along Rocky River Drive and Lorain Avenue.

Rental and sales prices are very affordable, with small bungalows going for less than $100,000. You'll pay more for a brick exterior or a house on the blocks west of Rocky River, but even the nicest houses rarely go for more than $200,000.

Groceries & Shopping

There's a Giant Eagle at Warren Village, 15325 Edgecliff Ave. In the same plaza is K & K Meats, which meat-eaters call one of the city's best butchers.

Marc's has a store in the treeless plaza at Kamm's Corners, 17400 Lorain Ave., with limited produce and discount dry goods. Discount Drug Mart, 17815 Puritas Ave., has a similar business model. (Giant Eagle and Marc's also have second locations further east on Lorain, in Westown – see box, p. 189.)

The Kamm's Corners Farmers Market is one of the larger markets in the city and happens on Sundays from 10 a.m. to 2 p.m. in the parking lot behind Walgreen's at 16906 Albers Ave., Bands and craftspeople add to the festive atmosphere. (The market moves indoors and happens once a month from November to May.)

Jasmine Bakery, 16700 Lorain Ave., is a neighborhood favorite; the owners not only bake pita bread and other Middle Eastern fare, but also run a small market where you can buy olives, canned goods and limited produce. Seven Seas Seafood, 15725 Lorain Ave., has fresh and frozen fish.

For pharmacy and toiletries, there's a Walgreen's Pharmacy at 16803 Lorain Ave. in addition to the Discount Drug Mart. The neighborhood also has a K Mart at 14901 Lorain Ave.

For specialty shopping, the aforementioned Lorain Triskett bike shop deserves mention, as does the skateboard shop Skater's Edge at 16211 Lorain Ave. Gino's Shoe Repair, 17116 Lorain Ave., can fix your shoes. Perhaps more fun are Carol & John's Comic Shop, 17462 Lorain Ave. at Kamm's Plaza, the last brick-and-mortar comic book shop in the city (though Big Fun also sells a more limited selection); and Starship Earth, a costume and novelty shop at 16880 Lorain Ave.

The West Park branch of the Cleveland Public Library is in a historic building at 3805 W. 157th St. near Lorain Ave.

Health & Recreation

West Park is blessed with a big range of options for staying healthy and active. The most beautiful – and probably the most popular – of these is the Cleveland MetroParks' Rocky River Reservation, at the neighborhood's far western border. The 2,000-acre park nestles in the dramatic Rocky River valley, hemmed in by huge shale cliffs. You'll find paved bicycling and walking trails, picnic areas, a dog park and places to launch kayaks and canoes. Rocky River is also known for having some of the best fly fishing in the region because of the runs of steelhead trout swimming to Lake Erie. Points of access are limited because of the topography; the only entrance from West Park proper is behind Fairview Hospital where Lorain Avenue hits the valley.

Impett Park is a large city park at 3207 W. 153rd St. The chief attractions here are ball fields and a pool, which are always hopping in the summer. Otherwise it's a fairly arid and sun-baked place.

Another city park, Gunning Park, lies further south at 16700 Puritas Ave. It's home to Gunning Recreation Center, one of the largest city-maintained recreation centers. The weight rooms and fitness classes are all free for city residents.

The neighborhood also has West Park YMCA, 15501 Lorain Ave., with a pool and the usual assortment of equipment and classes; check for fees and schedules. A private gym, Pro Fitness Center at 16602 Lorain Ave., draws old-school weightlifters.

The Sisters of St. Joseph runs River's Edge, 3430 Rocky River Dr. The lovely campus overlooks the Rocky River Valley and offers yoga and wellness classes, as well as spiritual retreats.

The campus of Fairview Hospital, a branch hospital of The Cleveland Clinic, lies just west of Kamm's Plaza on Lorain Avenue. You can see specialists here if you get sick, or visit the independent doctors' offices in the blocks around.

You can take your sick pet, meanwhile, to West Park Animal Hospital, 4117 Rocky River Dr.

Eating & Drinking Out

West Park's restaurants mostly serve the immediate neighborhood and surrounding suburbs. There are few – if any – destination spots as in Tremont, Downtown and Shaker Square, meaning the places that are here have a cozy, unpretentious feel.

Gene's Place to Dine, 3730 Rocky River Dr., has one of my favorite restaurant names in town. It has been serving up old-fashioned breakfasts, lunches and dinners for decades, its walls crowded with pictures of old celebrities and athletes.

The local Italian chain Panini's has a Kamm's Corners location, 17209 Lorain Ave. Si Senor, 16800 Lorain Ave., serves Mexican food for gringos. Each of these ethnic cuisines are better represented in neighboring Westown, just to the east, but they'll do in a pinch.

The neighborhood bars are Irish, Irish, Irish. These have a regional pull for Northeast Ohio's Irish-Americans, and become full to bursting on weekends. (Be advised: On weekend nights after 10 p.m., they tend to become rowdy hook-up joints for 20-somethings. Depending on your perspective, this could be a plus or a minus.) The two best-known are P.J. McIntyre's, 17119 Lorain Ave., and The Public House, 17219 Lorain Ave.

High school kids from all over the West Side congregate at Common Grounds, 17104 Lorain Ave., because of its late hours. The place has a gritty, vaguely punk rock vibe. Meanwhile, Savor the Moment, 4080 Rocky River Dr., has a die-hard customer base of older neighborhood residents. If you're looking for a chain, there's a Dunkin' Donuts at 16204 Lorain Ave.

West Park: The Once Over

It would be exhausting to see all of West Park on a single walking tour, but sticking to the area around Kamm's Corners will give you a feel for the neighborhood as a whole.

Start at Kamm's Plaza, at the intersection of Rocky River Drive and Lorain Avenue. Peek into the Marc's to get a sense of what's on offer there, and then – if you have even the slightest interest in comics – check out Carol & John's Comic Shop. From the plaza, walk west on Lorain Avenue to Fairview Hospital. Just beyond and to the south of the main campus, you'll see the twisty road that takes you down to the MetroParks' Rocky River Reservation. If you have an extra half hour or so, you can walk down to the park; otherwise, if you have a car or a bike, you should check it out on your way out.

Double back, walking on the south side of Lorain Avenue past Steak 'n Shake, The Public House and Panini's. Cross busy Rocky River Drive and continue east on Lorain. (To orient you: The Cleveland airport lies a couple miles to the South on Rocky River Drive.) You'll pass PJ McIntyre's and an assortment of other bars. Stop at the next cross-street, W. 158th St. There are some useful amenities (e.g. the YMCA, Seven Seas Seafood, the library and K-Mart) west of here, but the streetscape descends into drabness and becomes uninviting for pedestrians.

Cross to the north side of Lorain Avenue at W. 158th, and stop in to Jasmine Bakery if you're feeling peckish or just curious. Double back toward Rocky River Drive. You'll pass Si Senor, Starship Earth, Common Grounds and Gino's Shoe Repair.

At Rocky River Drive, turn right (North). Walk about a half-mile north. On your way, you'll pass side streets like Oxford Avenue and West Park Avenue and Our Lady of Angels Church, 3644 Rocky River Dr., which has an elementary school. At Greenwood Avenue, you'll see the Monastery of the Poor Clares Monastery, 3501 Rocky River Dr., on your right. This is home to a community of cloistered nuns who bake communion bread for local Catholic churches.

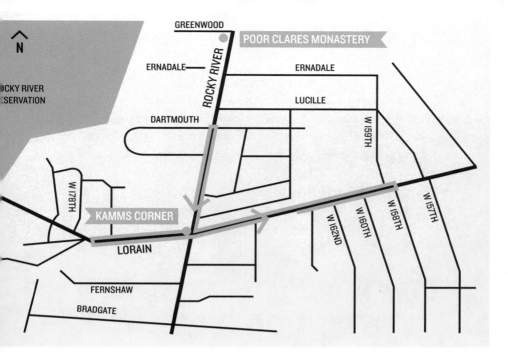

From here, double back on Rocky River toward Lorain. Wander down any of the side streets to get a taste of housing options. The nicest blocks are probably Greenwood Avenue and Ernadale Avenue west of Rocky River Drive. West Park, Lucille and Dartmouth avenues east of Rocky River Drive offer more modest – but still very nice – homes.

Back at the intersection of Rocky River and Lorain, stop in for a rest at any of the pubs or cafes, or a meal at Gene's Place to Dine if you'd like to absorb some local color.

WESTOWN

Westown is the more ethnically diverse cousin of West Park. It borders West Park immediately to the east, has similar housing stock and shares many of West Park's amenities (YMCA, grocery, etc.). Yet unlike predominantly white West Park, Westown's population is a mix of white, black, Middle Eastern and Latino. This diversity is apparent in the storefronts along Lorain Avenue, its main drag, between West Boulevard and W. 140th St. You're as likely to see signs in Arabic as English, and other ethnic establishments are present, too, making it one of the most intriguing – and least known – corners of the city.

Westown, like West Park, began life as an Irish neighborhood in the early 20th century. It has a typical Cleveland mix of single-families, doubles and apartment buildings. Most are in good repair, and housing prices are even lower here than in West Park, making it a popular landing point for new immigrants. The nicest houses are on West Boulevard; these were built to a grander scale, and on bigger lots, than most of the rest of the neighborhood.

The closest Rapid station is the Red Line Triskett station. This isn't an easy walk to or from Lorain Avenue – the distance is about a mile – but you could use it as a park- or bike-and-ride. Highway access is easy, with I-90 having interchanges at W. 117th St. and W. 140th St, and access to I-71 available at W. 130th Street and W. 150th Street.

There's a conglomeration of big box stores – surrounded by asphalt moats of parking – at I-90's interchange with W. 117th Street, along with a 24-hour Giant Eagle supermarket, 3050 W. 117th St. Giant Eagle has another, smaller location at 13820 Lorain Ave., and there's a Marc's discount variety and grocery store, at 5841 W. 130th St.

The Cleveland Public Library operates a branch at 11602 Lorain Ave., in the eastern part of the neighborhood. There's some random retail along this section of Lorain, too. Thrift shoppers swear by Value World, in the shopping plaza at 10694 Lorain Ave. And if you're the crafty type, Pat Catan's Art & Craft Supply, hidden in an industrial park at 12775 Berea Rd., has a huge selection of inexpensive supplies. Old-school Schindler's Fabric Shop, 9333 Lorain Ave., sells upholstery and curtain fabric.

The neighborhood's star attractions are its ethnic restaurants and markets. Some of the best are the delicious Luchita's Mexican Restaurant, 3456 W. 117th St.; Mi Pueblo Taqueria, 12207 Lorain Ave.; the original location of Phnom Penh (Cambodian), 13124 Lorain Ave.; and Der Braumeister (German), 13046 Lorain Ave., with a small import store inside.

Among Middle Eastern establishments, there's Sahara Restaurant, 12501 Lorain Ave. Caffé Roma, 13000 Lorain Ave., offers Italian baked goods and snacks. Deserving of special mention is the Salvadoran restaurant Pupuseria La Benedicion, 3685 W. 105th St. This little café in a bland strip mall is like a secret portal teleporting you directly to El Salvador. You can eat gooey pupusas (stuffed corn tortillas) while histrionic Mexican soap operas blare from the television in the corner.

The neighborhood has been working hard to redevelop the Variety Theatre, at Lorain and W. 121st St., into a special event space. Leaders have raised some funding, but at present it sits vacant.

Pupuseria "La Benedicion"

LAKE-WOOD

AND

CLEVELAND HEIGHTS

The Root Café in Lakewood

day 20/100

LAKEWOOD AND CLEVELAND HEIGHTS

—

When I was growing up in the 1980s and 1990s, the City proper seemed to have so little going for it that – ironically – many people wanting an urban experience in Cleveland lived in two of its suburbs: Lakewood and Cleveland Heights.

Both of these places grew up during the 1920s and 1930s. They have storefront districts built during the era of the streetcar. Their layouts are urban, with Lakewood in particular continuing the dense street grid of Cleveland proper.

Today, they continue to be attractive, urbane places. They have an air of greater affluence than most neighborhoods in the city proper, with better-maintained housing stock and fewer vacant storefronts. Understandably, many newcomers continue to choose these places when deciding where to live.

Yet the fact that they are suburbs creates some inconveniences. You won't be able to vote for Cleveland mayor, for example, or on any other issues affecting the city proper. And you'll be missing out on the crackle of energy that's uplifting many Cleveland neighborhoods around Downtown and University Circle. They are also farther from the city center than most Cleveland neighborhoods, meaning you'll spend a little longer traveling Downtown by car or public transit than if you lived in the city. In fact, Cleveland Heights has surprisingly poor transit options overall, with a trip Downtown entailing a rambling bus ride or a long walk to the Cedar-University Rapid Station. On the other hand, Cleveland Heights is a breeze of a commute to University Circle – just a few miles, and with some good bus connections.

April is
national
poetry month

Items are due on the   dates listed bel

Title: Bagration, 1944 : the destruction of
 Group C
Author: Zaloga, Steve.
Item ID: 0000612879353
Date due: 6/29/2021,23:59

Title: EU-MAIN UNCATALOGED MAGAZINE MARCH 20
Item ID: 0000624431201
Date due: 6/29/2021,23:59

Title: EU-MAIN UNCATALOGED MAGAZINE JUNE 202
Item ID: 0000624517090
Date due: 6/29/2021,23:59

Title: EU-MAIN UNCATALOGED MAGAZINE MAY 2021
Item ID: 0000624437836
Date due: 6/29/2021,23:59

Title: New to Cleveland : a guide to (re)dis
 ring the
Author: Glanville, Justin.
Item ID: 0000621004183
Date due: 6/29/2021,23:59

Title: Your perfect nursery : a step-by-step
 roach to
Author: Coe, Naomi.
Item ID: 0000624754453
Date due: 6/29/2021,23:59

Euclid Public Library

Total Items: 6
Date Printed: 6/8/2021 1:46:42 PM

e
Euclid Public Library
216-261-5300
Adult Department press 3
Children's Department press 4
Renew Items press 2
Employee Directory press 9

Visit us on the web: www.euclidlibrary.org

Phoenix Coffee on Coventry

day 24/100

For some people, of course, those very qualities – a sense of remove, stability over dynamism– will be attractors. The best way to get a sense of your own preference is to walk the places in this book that call out to you most.

CLEVELAND HEIGHTS

Cleveland Heights borders Cleveland just East of University Circle. The city's upper classes have always tended to drift East rather than West, and this was one of the first places they went after leaving their mansions on Euclid Avenue. The grandest homes are on Fairmount Boulevard, east of Cedar Road – huge stone and brick piles with six or more bedrooms.

But most parts of "The Heights" (local parlance not just for Cleveland Heights but also neighboring Shaker Heights and University Heights) are more modest. There are many wonderful old wood-frame houses in good repair, on leafier, more generous lots than you'll find in either the city or in Lakewood.

Cleveland Heights has a brainy, East Coast feel, due both to its moneyed pedigree and its proximity to the academic and cultural institutions of University Circle. The place has always been popular with students, professors, members of the Cleveland Orchestra and artists. It's sometimes called "The People's Republic of Cleveland Heights" because of its ultra-liberal politics. It prides itself on being a diverse community, and the population is about half white and half black – though as in the region as a whole, boundaries between the "white" and "black" parts of town are distinct. (For example, in the Coventry district, whites tend to live south of Mayfield Road, while blacks live north.) The public high school has become nearly 90 percent black, indicating that many white families are either moving away before their kids reach ninth grade or sending their kids to private schools.

The residential districts cluster around one of six retail nodes. The most famous of these is Coventry Road, about a mile and a half uphill from University Circle. The three blocks or so between Euclid Heights Boulevard and Mayfield Road have long had a Bohemian air. Although the district has become more mainstream since the 1990s, it's still one of the best places in the region to shop, eat and watch people. Tommy's Restaurant, 1824 Coventry Rd., is here, serving a huge menu of gloppy but delicious comfort food. It has many vegetarian options. You'll also find Big Fun vintage store, 1814 Coventry Rd. and the only Northeast Ohio location of American Apparel, 1782 Coventry Rd. Utrecht Art Supplies runs a location at 2768 Mayfield Rd., and a branch of the excellent Cleveland Heights Public Library is at 1925 Coventry Rd.

Cedar Lee Theater day 27/100

Vintage apartment buildings – some of them now condos – line Euclid Heights Boulevard and Hampshire Road. Lovely old homes, most in good condition, pack the blocks surrounding Coventry. The unspectacular but cheap Marc's, 1833 Coventry Rd., is the only walkable place to buy groceries, though there's also a farmer's market on Thursday nights in the summer, 6 to 9 p.m., at 1824 Coventry Rd., and there are many options a few miles away if you're willing to drive.

The intersection of Cedar and Lee roads, another two miles east, is the second liveliest part of town, and boasts a more complete lineup of amenities. Here you'll find the venerable Cedar-Lee Theatre, 2163 Lee Rd., which shows independent films. There's a slew of restaurants, of which the favorites include Lopez y Gonzalez, 2196 Lee Rd. and Anatolia Café (Turkish), 2270 Lee Rd. The main branch of the Cleveland Heights Public Library is at 2345 Lee Rd. One of the best independent grocery stores in the region, Zagara's Market, is at 1940 Lee Rd. Houses are mostly comfortable single-families and doubles, though there are a few apartment buildings around Meadowbrook Road. Phoenix Coffee, 2287 Lee Rd., and The Stone Oven Bakery, 2267 Lee Rd., are beloved.

Cedar-Fairmount – named after the intersection of its main streets – is sometimes called "The Upper East Side" of Cleveland Heights. It's the closest district in Cleveland Heights to University Circle – about a mile from the University-Cedar Rapid station. The houses on surrounding streets, especially Fairmount Boulevard, are among the stateliest in the region and some fetch $1 million or more. There are apartment buildings and condos, too. Within walking distance are a Starbucks, 12405 Cedar Rd.; Bruegger's Bagels, 12443 Cedar Rd.; the independent Appletree Books, 12419 Cedar Rd.; the popular Mad Greek restaurant, 2466 Fairmount Blvd.; and Aladdin's Eatery (Middle Eastern), 12447 Cedar Rd. There's a Dave's Supermarket at 12438 Cedar Rd.

At Mayfield and Lee roads, the Rockefeller Building has a Starbucks, some upscale gift shops and Rockefeller's restaurant, 3099 Mayfield Rd., in a spectacular old ballroom.

More sedate and farther flung are the districts around Fairmount Boulevard and Taylor Road and around Cedar and Taylor roads. The former is popular among students at nearby John Carroll University. The latter is the center of an Orthodox Jewish community, though some of its institutions have recently moved to the farther suburb of Beachwood. Both, coincidentally, are home to wonderful bakeries. On the Rise, 3471 Fairmount Blvd., bakes delicious artisan loaves, while Unger's, 1831 S. Taylor Rd., has kosher ryes. There's also a great, creative Chinese restaurant, Sun Luck Garden, at 1901 S. Taylor Rd. Be sure to take time to chat with Sun Luck's friendly owner, Annie Chiu.

Cleveland Heights' main parks are Cain Park, 14591 Superior Rd., which has an outdoor amphitheater that hosts summer concerts; and Shaker Lakes (see p. 163), which you can access at the intersection of Coventry Road and North Park Boulevard. The city has big box shopping (Home Depot, Walmart, etc.) and a Bally's gym at Severance Town Center, at the intersection of Mayfield and Taylor roads.

Cleveland Heights and surrounding suburbs fought the construction of freeways through their neighborhoods in the 1960s and 1970s. The most famous fight was one against the so-called Clark Freeway, which would have obliterated the Shaker Lakes. The happy result is that neighborhoods here are whole and intact, with no unsightly freeway overpasses and entrance ramps. The trade-off is that freeway access is difficult, with I-90 and I-480 many stoplights away. Most residents consider this a small price to pay, but if your commute requires you to travel the freeways, the Heights may be a frustrating place to live.

LAKEWOOD

Lakewood, directly west of the Cleveland neighborhood of Edgewater, has a scruffier, more Midwestern vibe. With a population of some 50,000 in about six square miles, it is said to be the most densely populated American city between New York and Chicago. There are some grand houses on Clifton and Lake boulevards, but on the whole the stock isn't much different from what you'll find in the city proper: generous single-families, doubles and apartment buildings on small lots.

The major exception to this rule is the Gold Coast, in the northeast corner of the city near the shore of Lake Erie. Here you'll find perhaps half a dozen high-rise condo buildings with spectacular views of the lake and Downtown. Most date from the 1950s through the 1970s. Despite the area's name, it's not very expensive to live here, with many condos available for less than $100,000.

The city has a more linear layout than Cleveland Heights. Its streets run like rungs of a ladder off the main arteries of Lake, Clifton, Detroit and Madison avenues. Detroit and Madison are the main commercial thoroughfares.

In general, Lakewood becomes more affluent the farther west you go, and the housing and retail reflect this. Used car lots and a few rag-tag nightclubs mar the East End from Detroit Avenue south, though the city has made efforts to revive this area with new townhomes.

The intersection of Detroit Avenue and Warren Road – known as Downtown Lakewood – is positively bustling. It's possible to live in this area and have little need for a car. Within a few blocks you can walk to a Giant Eagle grocery store, 14100 Detroit Ave.; Geiger's Clothing & Sports, 14710 Detroit Ave.; a shopping plaza with a Marc's and other stores; the fantastic Lakewood Public Library, 15425 Detroit Ave.; and a bevy of cafes and restaurants. (If you need to get somewhere else, though, the number 26 bus on Detroit is notoriously slow on its route to Downtown, and the closest Rapid stations are several miles south in the Cleveland neighborhood of West Park.)

This area has the wonderful Root Café, 15118 Detroit Ave., which serves great coffee and vegetarian food, including a to-die-for tempeh-pesto sandwich. Also good for vegetarians is Szechwan Garden, 13800 Detroit Ave., which has plenty of dishes featuring meat substitutes (though real meat is an option as well). Melt Bar and Grilled, 14718 Detroit Ave., serves beer and gourmet grilled cheese sandwiches and has been a sensation since its opening in 2005. Expect a wait of an hour or more for a table at dinner time. (There's a Cleveland Heights location, 13463 Cedar Rd., that's less competitive.) Deagan's Kitchen & Bar, 14810 Detroit Ave., has won a loyal following for its 21st century take on pub grub. Down on Madison Avenue are Angelo's Pizza, 13715 Madison Ave., which many consider to serve the best pies in Cleveland, and an old-fashioned Malley's shop, 13401 Madison Ave., which serves ice cream and locally made chocolate.

The Rocky River Metropark

day 76/100

LOCATION

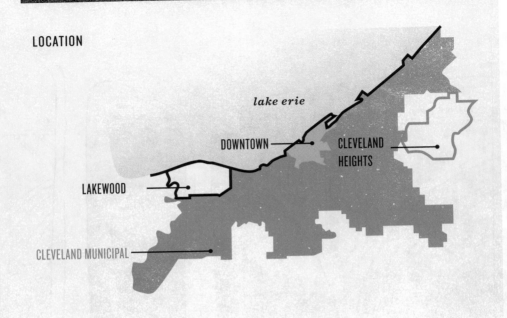

lake erie

DOWNTOWN

CLEVELAND HEIGHTS

LAKEWOOD

CLEVELAND MUNICIPAL

The West End of Lakewood is the most affluent part of town. Here you'll find yoga and pilates studios, including Puma Yoga, 15602 Detroit Ave. and Acenda Yoga, 17305 Madison Ave., both excellent; the friendly independent Pet's General Store, 16821 Madison Ave.; and bakeries such as the great Breadsmith, 18101 Detroit Ave., and Blackbird Baking Co., 1391 Sloane Ave. India Garden, 18405 Detroit Ave., serves above-average Indian food.

Residents in this area also benefit from close proximity to the Rocky River Reservation of the Cleveland MetroParks, at the western edge of Lakewood at the intersection of Detroit Avenue and Valley Parkway. The park offers paved walking and biking trails through the Rocky River valley, a dog run and is immaculately maintained. Also notable in this part of town is Nature's Bin, 18120 Sloane Ave., a nonprofit grocery store with nice organic produce and bulk goods. It has a job training program for mentally disabled people.

Cleveland house interior, The Mojher DeLucca house day 37/100

Apart from the MetroParks reservation, Lakewood doesn't have much green space.
Most of the Lakewood lakefront is private. One of the few exceptions is Lakewood Park,
14532 Lake Ave., a small city park with walking paths and great views of Downtown
and Lake Erie. Lakewood is (in)famous for the dozens of bars – many of them Irish-themed
– that line Detroit and Madison avenues. These are popular with the many Cleveland State
University students and recent college graduates who call Lakewood home. The bars
can get rambunctious on weekends, with knots of patrons spilling out onto sidewalks
to smoke. Typical of these is the Put-in-Bay, 18206 Detroit Ave., with its gaudy Lake Erie
Islands décor; Around the Corner, 18616 Detroit Ave.; and the West End Tavern, 18515
Detroit Ave. For the older, more sedate crowd, there's Bela Dubby, 13321 Madison Ave.,
and Mars Bar, 15314 Madison Ave.

Around the holidays, artists with studios in the Lakewood Screw Factory, 13000
Athens Rd., open their spaces to shoppers.

SETTLING IN

You've picked a neighborhood — now what? This section will help you get settled and oriented.

TRANSPORTATION IN CLEVELAND

Driving

Many Clevelanders (around 30% of the population) get by without a car, either due to economic factors or because they choose to live a car-free lifestyle. However, most Northeast Ohioans with means get around by car. The reasons for this are complex, but here are some of the most important:

Cars are part of both Cleveland's and Ohio's culture. Cars are manufactured all over the state, with Northeast Ohio serving as a hub for the manufacture of car parts. Going as far back as the early 20th century, owning a car here has been not just a statement of personal freedom, but of supporting local manufacturers.

We have highways coming out our ears, making it quick and easy to drive anywhere you want to go. The region saw a massive shift to the suburbs after World War II, due to a mix of racial tension and readily available land. State and federal governments cooperated by building an enormous network of roads and freeways. At the time, Cleveland was one of the ten largest cities in the nation, and had a geographic location at an important transportation crossroads. So it got an especially large freeway system – one that seems almost ridiculously outsized today. Traffic, even during rush hour, is some of the lightest in the nation.

It's very easy to park. Because so many people drive, there's insatiable demand for parking. To remain economically viable, merchants and employers and even the City of Cleveland itself have felt compelled to build and maintain convenient and ample parking, often immediately adjacent to destinations.

Public transportation is set up mostly for commuting to Downtown. All buses terminate at Public Square Downtown, so to get from one side of town to the other will require a transfer. Meanwhile, a lot of jobs are now located in the suburbs instead of Downtown. To travel to suburban employment centers like Beachwood or Independence without a car can be an hours-long ordeal.

In general, hubs of activity are spread far apart. This is especially true between far-flung suburbs, but there are wide gulfs even between city neighborhoods. Detroit Shoreway, for example, lies eight miles away from University Circle. This rules out walking for just about everyone, and even on a bicycle it's not an insignificant distance. Even shorter gaps – like the one-mile dead zone between Ohio City and Tremont – seem longer than they are because of vacant lots and blank spaces.

The weather is cold in the winter. In case you hadn't heard, Cleveland has tough winters. For most people, it's more comfortable to hop into a heated car than to walk or bicycle, or to shiver at an outdoor Rapid or bus station. (The flip side, of course, is the danger of driving on ice-slick roads.)

All that said, Cleveland is a lot more amenable to non-automotive travel than many cities in the United States. If you're thoughtful, you can set up a life where you don't need to drive to work, and where you're within walking distance of most of your daily necessities. If you work and live Downtown, for example, you'll probably find yourself managing without a car for most of the work week. The same would hold true if you lived and worked in University Circle. Working from home, meanwhile, means you could live in a place like Ohio City or Shaker Square and be able to do most of your shopping and socializing within the neighborhood. Living in either of those neighborhoods means you'll also have good transit options to Downtown.

And some people do in fact live car-free in Cleveland. Theirs is not the most convenient existence. But between their bicycles, public transportation, the kindness of friends willing to give them rides and the occasional cab, these intrepid souls make it work.

The Rand Green line train

day 26/100

Public Transportation

The Greater Cleveland Regional Transit Authority (RTA) runs public transportation throughout Cuyahoga County. Its buses connect with transit authorities in surrounding counties, such as Lorain, Summit and Lake, if you need to get farther afield.

Buses are the predominant form of public transportation in Cleveland, but there are also three train lines: the Red, Blue and Green. The local (and I think pretty cute) name for the train is "the Rapid" – short for Rapid Transit – as in, "Has the Rapid come yet?" All three lines converge at Tower City in Downtown Cleveland, and follow the same route from there to E. 55th Street. Tower City and E. 55th are the most convenient transfer points.

Rapid trains don't operate on the same scale as subway systems in denser cities like New York or Washington. There are big distances between stops – several miles in some cases. Also, the trains run in former freight rail right-of-ways, so the stops (at least in the city proper) are sometimes inconveniently located at the edge of neighborhoods rather than in the center. For example, the W. 65th St. station is about a mile from the action at W. 65th and Detroit Avenue in Detroit Shoreway.

To its credit, RTA has tried to encourage dense development around key stops – especially along the Red Line. It also has plans to move one station, at E. 120th Street and Euclid Avenue, to the more densely populated intersection of Mayfield and Random roads in Little Italy. But lack of funding and the soft real estate market have kept these efforts mostly in the planning stages.

The Red Line is the most useful for most people, and it's the only bus or Rapid line in the city that goes all the way across town. It runs from Cleveland Hopkins International Airport, on the far West Side, to the inner-ring suburb of East Cleveland on the East Side. Along the way, it stops in or around the neighborhoods of West Park, Edgewater, Detroit Shoreway, Ohio City, Downtown and University Circle/Little Italy. It runs every 15 minutes; more often during rush hour. Trains run from 3 a.m. until 1 a.m.

Most of the people who ride the Blue and Green lines are on their way between Downtown and Shaker Square or Shaker Heights. These trains follow the same route from Downtown to Shaker Square; on the way, you'll pass through some of the most depopulated parts of the city, and few people get on or off the train between E. 55th Street and Shaker Square. At Shaker Square, the lines diverge. The Green Line covers the northern part of Shaker Heights and the Blue Line covers the southern part. Each line runs about every 30 minutes, in 15-minute staggered increments, but more often during rush hour. Trains start running at 5 a.m. and go until midnight.

The new Health Line, unveiled in 2007, is a bus that imitates a train. Large, articulated buses run along Euclid Avenue from Downtown to East Cleveland via Cleveland State University and University Circle. The buses stop at dedicated, enclosed stations. You pay your fare at the stations, rather than on the bus, helping to speed travel times. RTA says it takes 15 minutes to get from Downtown to University Circle, though riders report that it can take much longer, especially during rush hour. The line was coupled with major streetscape renovations along Euclid Avenue – bicycle lanes, new trees, wider sidewalks, public art. To date it's been a huge success, exceeding projected ridership rates, and has spurred new private investment along its route.

There are lots of conventional buses, too, but they're generally much slower than trains and the Health Line because they make so many stops. None of them go all the way across town, so if you're going from the West Side to the East Side you'll be making a transfer – most likely at Public Square Downtown – and the journey could be epic. RTA posts schedules on its website to help you plan trips between given points.

Combining bicycling with transit can save time. All RTA buses are equipped with bike racks on their snouts, and you can take bikes on Rapid trains except during rush hour.

Like so many elements of life in Cleveland, public transit has become mixed up with tension around race and class. More affluent Clevelanders regard buses and trains (especially buses) as being only for people who are too poor to own cars. And, in fact, if you take transit you will encounter lots of people who are down on their luck; some may smell not so great or ask you for change. Meanwhile, some white suburbanites regard buses and trains as being only for blacks. To be a committed transit rider, you will have to rise above these misconceptions and prejudices.

RTA has been hamstrung by a dearth of funding from the state of Ohio in recent years. The state is among the nation's least supportive of transit, spending about one-thirtieth the amount per capita as Pennsylvania and one-tenth the amount as Michigan. The result has been an increase in fares and a reduction in bus routes. The fare for all buses and trains is now $2.25 per ride, though you can also buy daily and monthly passes.

Bicycling

Bicycling culture is booming in Cleveland. Lower-income people who can't afford cars have been bicycling to work and to run errands for years. But pedaling is also gaining popularity among white, professional class folks who want to get more exercise or reduce their carbon footprints. The city is still far behind places like Chicago or Portland, but on streets like Euclid Avenue and Detroit Avenue you'll see a growing number of two-wheeled commuters during rush hours.

The city has cooperated by marking bicycle lanes along most of Euclid Avenue and on two of the major crosstown bridges (the Lorain-Carnegie and Detroit-Superior), and by painting "sharrows" (share the road arrows) on Franklin Boulevard. There's also a new, city-sponsored bike station Downtown, called The Bike Rack, for those who want to lock up their bikes and shower after commuting to work. The Bike Rack is located at 2148 E. 4th St., south of Prospect Avenue.

You can download bicycling maps, recommending the best routes for bicyclists through the city and surrounding suburbs, from the Web site of the Northeast Ohio Areawide Coordinating Agency (NOACA) at www.noaca.org/bikemaps.html. In a sign of cycling's rising popularity, several new bicycle shops have opened in the city in the last few years. North Collinwood, Detroit Shoreway, Ohio City and Tremont all have relatively new shops.

The city also has a monthly Critical Mass ride, in which 200 or more cyclists follow a given route through town, often with drinks afterward. The event isn't as militant as it is in some cities, but it has succeeded in bringing new visibility to bicycle culture – and is one of the most fun and social regular events in town. Search "Cleveland Critical Mass" on Facebook for more information.

THE BEST CAR-FREE AND CAR-LIGHT NEIGHBORHOODS IN CLEVELAND

1. Downtown. Two small grocery stores, gyms, restaurants, bars and access to practically every bus and Rapid line in the city. Plus, it's the largest employment center in the region, meaning you have a good chance of being able to walk to work.

2. Ohio City. The West Side Market, Dave's Supermarket, specialty shops and restaurants and the second-largest transit hub in the city with access to both the Red Line Rapid and several buses.

3. Shaker Square. All-year farmers' market, Dave's Supermarket, specialty shops and restaurants and the Blue and Green Rapid lines to Downtown.

4. University Circle/Little Italy. The Rapid Red Line, restaurants and tons of culture just steps away, plus it's the region's second largest hub for jobs. May move up the list once Uptown comes online with a grocery store.

5. Tie: Detroit Shoreway, Tremont, Edgewater, Cedar-Fairmount, Coventry, Cedar-Lee, Downtown Lakewood. All of these neighborhoods lack certain essential amenities (a decent grocery store in Detroit Shoreway and Coventry, for example), and/or have few transit options. But they are dense and urban and you could get by for most of the week without a car.

Flying

Cleveland Hopkins International Airport lies only about 13 miles from Downtown Cleveland. Connected to the city's heart by the Red Line Rapid and with easy highway access via I-71 and I-480, it's among the most accessible airports in the nation.

For decades, Continental Airlines has operated a secondary hub here, with direct flights to dozens of cities on the East Coast and in the Midwest, and to a few on the West Coast. Direct flights to Mexico (Cancun), Puerto Rico and Canada (Montreal, Toronto and Ottawa) have also been available. (From Cleveland, it's about an hour to most cities on the East Coast, about five hours to the West, not including stopovers.)

The future of Continental's Cleveland hub is unclear. The airline is in the process of merging with United Airlines, and United has a major hub a short distance away in Chicago. This could spell a reduction in travel options from Cleveland once the merger is complete in 2012.

Most other major airlines offer flights between Cleveland and their hubs. Budget airlines operate out of Hopkins as well. Southwest Airlines, for example, offers low-cost flights to Baltimore/Washington, Chicago and Florida. If you can find a way to the Akron/Canton airport, about an hour from Cleveland by car, you can catch budget flights on AirTran to Atlanta, Boston, Florida and New York.

Long-Distance Trains and Buses

Amtrak operates trains to Chicago, New York and Washington from Cleveland. But to catch one, you'll need to find your way to an obscure corner of Downtown in the middle of the night. The station is on the lakefront, near the Rock and Roll Hall of Fame, at 200

East Memorial Parkway. Amtrak operates all of its long-distance trains from the East Coast to Chicago overnight, which means that trains arrive in Cleveland at ungodly hours like 3 a.m. or 5 a.m. Also, be forewarned that Amtrak is notorious for delays on its long-distance routes, because passenger trains have to defer to freight traffic. The Greyhound station is located near the campus of Cleveland State University, on the east edge of Downtown, at 1465 Chester Ave. The building is very cool, a 1940s-era Moderne structure, but the inside is fluorescent-lit and dispiriting in the way of most Greyhound hubs. From here you can catch buses to cities on the East Coast and in the Midwest.

MegaBus, a newer operator, runs budget buses from Cleveland to Chicago and Pittsburgh. If you buy your tickets far enough in advance, the fare can be as low as $1 each way – though you'll have to book most of a year ahead to get those prices. More typical costs are in the range of $15 to $30 each way. The buses are wildly popular, but "getting what you pay for" can certainly apply. The one time I tried MegaBus, the bus ran out of gas – yep, you read that right – about 30 minutes outside of Chicago. We Cleveland refugees had to pack on to another bus coming from another city about an hour later. Buses leave from behind Tower City on Huron Road and run twice a day.

ARTS & CULTURE

One of Cleveland's chief assets is its embarrassment of cultural riches. Some cultural institutions – the awesome library system, the art museum, the orchestra – date back to the city's early 20th century industrial heyday. But there's also an active population of visual artists, writers, musicians and other creative types who thrive here today.

According to the Community Partnership for Arts and Culture (CPAC), Cleveland and its suburbs are home to a disproportionately high population of musicians, in particular – perhaps due to the region's strong classical and rock music heritage. But writers, visual artists and dancers abound, too.

A good way to get an overview of the city's cultural offerings during a given week is to check out the alternative weekly newspaper, Cleveland Scene, which has comprehensive listings. *The Cleveland Plain Dealer* also publishes a weekly insert, called Friday! Magazine, with listings, and the ezine CoolCleveland.com is very good, too.

VISUAL ARTS

The city has many museums and galleries. The Cleveland Museum of Art, 11150 East Blvd., will finish up a $500 million expansion in 2013, and is generally regarded as one of the great art museums in the U.S. There are few better ways to spend an afternoon – or a whole day – than wandering its galleries. Best of all, the museum is completely free (except special exhibits).

The Museum of Contemporary Art Cleveland (MOCA) will open a new building at the intersection of Mayfield Road and Euclid Avenue in 2012. It features rotating exhibits by contemporary artists from around the world. The building itself will be a kind of Rubik's cube-gone-bad – an asymmetrical box designed by Farshid Moussavi.

On the independent gallery scene, Tremont has a clutch of well-run spaces ranging from the gift shop-esque to the experimental. The neighborhood hosts an Art Walk on the second Friday night of every month; this is a good time to visit most of the galleries at once.

Meanwhile, artists in the loft buildings of Asiatown open their studios to visitors around the holidays. (See City Artists at Work, www.cityartistsatwork.org, for details.)

Two galleries downtown deserve special note: The Bonfoey Gallery, 1710 Euclid Ave., displays works by major contemporary artists; while the William Rupnik Gallery, 1117 Euclid Ave., has a more regional focus.

The Sculpture Center, on the edge of University Circle at 1834 E. 123rd St., hosts rotating sculpture exhibits. Students and faculty often show their work at the Cleveland Institute of Art, 11141 East Blvd., and at the Cleveland State University gallery, 2307 Chester Ave. CIA's industrial design program is among the best in the nation, and the annual exhibit of work by students and faculty in that program – usually in December – is a great place to find out how toothpaste tubes and cars will look in the future.

MUSIC

The Cleveland Orchestra has been stunning audiences around the world since George Szell was conductor in the 1950s. It's considered one of the "Big Five" orchestras in the U.S., and one of the best in the world. You can hear them play at their home in Severance Hall, 11001 Euclid Ave., in the spring, fall and winter. If you're a student, you can buy tickets for as little as $10 (with proper ID); normal seats in the upper balcony go for as little as $30. In the summer, they play a series of outdoor concerts at Blossom Music Center in Cuyahoga Valley National Park, where you can take a picnic and wine or beer. Lawn seats are around $20.

The Cleveland Opera is also well regarded. They typically perform at Playhouse Square, but even if you're not an opera fan, their annual (and free) outdoor summer concert at the Italian Cultural Garden in Rockefeller Park is not to be missed.

As for popular music, Cleveland audiences seem to have special tastes for two widely divergent styles. The first is American roots music – folk, blues and Americana. You could hear a different band in this genre every night at small places like The Winchester, 12112 Madison Ave. in Lakewood; Parkview Nite Club, 1261 W. 58th St.; The Barking Spider,

11310 Juniper Rd.; Brother's Lounge, 11607 Detroit Ave.; The Beachland Ballroom, 15417 Waterloo Rd.; and any number of coffee shops and restaurants around town.

At the opposite end of the volume knob, Clevelanders also love their punk, hardcore and metal – bands named, for example, after deadly diseases and vermin. Check the schedules of Peabody's, 2083 E. 21st St.; Now That's Class, 11213 Detroit Ave.; and Pat's in the Flats, 2233 W. 3rd St.

Cleveland doesn't draw the same variety of up-and-coming rock and pop bands as a Chicago or a Seattle, but there's still plenty to see. The best venues for indie acts and current critics' darlings (think Arcade Fire and The Decemberists before they were big) are the Beachland Ballroom and The Grog Shop, 2785 Euclid Heights Blvd. in Cleveland Heights. The Happy Dog, 5801 Detroit Ave., hosts local and regional acts trying to make it to the national stage – many of them quite good. You can find out about the best in live contemporary rock shows in Cleveland by checking out Roger Zender's excellent blog The Zender Agenda.

DANCE

Cleveland suffered a blow to its ego when The Cleveland Ballet dissolved about 10 years ago. But the concert series and local companies that have risen in the Ballet's absence have created a more diverse and perhaps more interesting scene.

Verb Ballets is the best-known of the local companies. They perform around town throughout the year, including an annual free concert in Tremont in August. Other troupes to look out for are Morrison Dance, Inlet, Groundworks and Dancing Wheels (which includes dancers in wheelchairs).

Dance lovers should check the offerings of Dance Cleveland, a group that sponors performances by major national troupes, often at Playhouse Square.

FILM

One of the city's most beloved events is the annual Cleveland International Film Festival. The festival has been running since 1976 and now attracts more than 70,000 filmgoers over the course of two weeks – usually in March. The quantity of films staggers, but especially strong are the offerings in Jewish, environmentally-themed and gay films. The festival happens Downtown, at Tower City Cinemas.

Other times of the year, you can catch foreign, art and revival films at the wonderful Cleveland Cinematheque at the Cleveland Institute of Art. Save your ticket stubs: The curator of the series, John Ewing, gives a wry, monotone speech at the start of each film and awards a gift certificate to a local bookstore or coffee shop. The Cleveland Museum of Art also shows international and off-beat films.

The Cedar-Lee Theatre in Cleveland Heights, and the Capitol Theatre in Detroit-Shoreway screen high-brow Hollywood fare. Mainstream multiplex cinemas are mostly in the suburbs, with two notable exceptions: Downtown's Tower City Cinemas and Shaker Square Cinemas.

THEATER

Both in the city proper and in the suburbs, Cleveland boasts a vibrant theater scene. The best-known local companies include the Cleveland Play House, the oldest regional repertory company in the nation; and Great Lakes Theatre Festival. Both troupes perform in the ornate 1920s theaters of Playhouse Square downtown, the Play House having recently moved from its original home near University Circle. Playhouse Square also hosts national touring acts.

Karamu House, nationally known for interracial productions, operates at 2355 E. 89th St. Cleveland Public Theatre, on a growing campus of spaces around 6415 Detroit Ave., stages experimental productions and runs programs to foster new playwrights. It also runs some outreach programs for homeless men and schoolchildren.

Smaller companies include Convergence Continuum, often staging plays at a church in Tremont; Ensemble Theatre, which performs in a former elementary school in the Coventry neighborhood of Cleveland Heights; Dobama Theatre Company, performing on Lee Road in Cleveland Heights; and Near West Theatre Company, which stages heartwarming (and often heartbreaking) full-scale musicals featuring youth from the city's near west side in Ohio City. (Near West hopes to build its own theater in Detroit Shoreway.) The Beck Center for the Performing Arts stages professional and youth theater productions in Lakewood.

CLEVELAND FOR ARTISTS

Cleveland doesn't have a reputation for being a hotbed of artistic activity – testament perhaps to its blue-collar heritage. But in fact, the arts scene in Cleveland is already thriving and continues to grow more vibrant by the day. The city's world-class cultural institutions and universities play a huge role, but also important is the sheer affordability of the place. An article in the *Wall Street Journal* in 2009 reported a trend of artists moving from expensive coastal cities like New York to cities like Cleveland to find cheap housing in an urban and supportive setting.

In 2011, CPAC started a new Artists' Housing program to support this trend. The program will offer grants and loan assistance for artists who want to buy a house in the city, with North Collinwood as the pilot neighborhood. If you're more interested in loft-style live-work space, see p. 27. The most popular neighborhoods for artists in Cleveland are Tremont, Ohio City, Detroit Shoreway, Asiatown, University Circle, Shaker Square/ Buckeye and North Collinwood; and the urban 'burbs of Lakewood and Cleveland Heights.

Perhaps even more enticingly, CPAC began offering grants to individual artists living in Cuyahoga County in 2009. Grants to individual artists are rare, and Cleveland's are some of the most generous in the country. The Creative Workforce Fellowship provides cash awards of $20,000 to each of about 20 artists in all disciplines. Arts nonprofits are well-funded by Cuyahoga Arts and Culture and other local foundations, and many of these organizations hire individual artists to produce work (see list below).

There are other great resources in town to support artists. The local Council of Smaller Enterprises (COSE) has an Arts Network program that connects artists with health insurance, for example. It also offers a training program called the Artist as an Entrepreneur Institute, which trains artists to run small businesses and market themselves. The Noteworthy Federal Credit Union provides banking and financial services targeted at artists. Volunteer Lawyers for Arts has a local chapter which provides free legal advice for artists (call the Cleveland Bar Association at 216-696-3525 for more information). A networking group, Cleveland Young Arts Professionals, organizes events around town; find them on Facebook.

Playhouse Square Center

day 87/100

The local nonprofit for writers, known as The LIT, is in the process of merging with the Cuyahoga County Public Library. Once the merger is complete, fiction and nonfiction writers will be able to enroll in free workshops at library branches around the county. (Cleveland is home to a bevy of well-known writers, including Thrity Umrigar, Dan Chaon, Paula McLain, Sarah Willis and Patricia Springstubb, some of whom teach workshops.)

There are many nonprofit organizations that provide networking and training opportunities for artists in all disciplines. To get a sense of the scene in your discipline before you arrive, you can check out the following:

- Artspace Cleveland (loft space for artists), *www.artspacecleveland.org*
- City Artists at Work, *www.cityartistsatwork.org*
- Cleveland Public Theatre, *www.cptonline.org*
- Dance Cleveland, *www.dancecleveland.org*
- Great Lakes Theatre Festival, *www.greatlakestheater.org*
- Greater Cleveland Film Commission, *www.clevelandfilm.com*
- The LIT (poets and writers), *www.the-lit.org*
- Ohio Independent Film Festival, *www.ohiofilms.com*
- Zygote Press (printmaking cooperative), *www.zygotepress.com*
- Music Cleveland, *www.musiccleveland.com*
- Cleveland Handmade, *www.clevelandhandmade.com*
- Cleveland Craft Coalition, on Facebook

Until recently, perhaps the biggest obstacle to artists living in Cleveland has been the real or perceived lack of a customer base. The tastes of Cleveland art consumers have always veered conservative – see the collection of the Art Museum. Yet appreciation for contemporary art, music and literature in Cleveland is growing. More important, the ease of selling art, music and literature online is erasing the need to be near more daring customers in New York and Los Angeles.

SHOPPING: AN OVERVIEW

Newcomers to Cleveland might be surprised by the apparent lack of retail in the city proper. This situation dates to the suburban boom of the 1950s and 1960s, when many residents with means left for greener pastures and retailers followed.

In many city neighborhoods, it can be difficult to meet your daily needs without at least occasional trips to another neighborhood or the suburbs. Almost every neighborhood is missing something – a pharmacy in Ohio City, for example, or a grocery store in Edgewater. Unfortunately, many Clevelanders have acclimated to driving long distances to meet their needs – an unsustainable system by most measures.

The good news is that more and more merchants – most of them independent – are seeing opportunity in city neighborhoods. New interest in urban living is driving some of the trend, but (ironically) the poor economy has also helped, since many laid-off employees are now seeking ways to support themselves. Since 2008 alone, a cadre of bike shops, clothing stores, bakeries and gift stores have opened in Tremont, Detroit Shoreway, Ohio City, North Collinwood and Downtown, with more on the way in University Circle. The trend is still new, but Cleveland finally seems to be getting into the independent retail groove. (See below for specific listings.)

For many neighborhoods, the biggest missing piece remains decent access to groceries and fresh produce. Much of the city's East Side, and big parts of the West Side, are so-called food deserts. These are areas with limited access to markets selling fresh produce. In food deserts, it's easier to find a McDonald's than a supermarket. A coalition of nonprofit and government groups is working to change this, and there's real momentum behind starting new neighborhood food stores thanks to the city's booming local food movement (see p. 92). In the meantime, though, you'll be stuck driving or taking the Rapid to full-service supermarkets if you live in some neighborhoods.

Many people will also find shopping for clothing to be a challenge, especially those accustomed to the broader and more downtown-focused scenes of larger cities. Experiments with downtown malls in Cleveland in the 1980s and 1990s mostly failed. The result has been that unless you're a big fan a thrift shops, you'll likely find yourself

Blackbird Baking Company

day 18/100 *(See p. 202)*

trekking out to malls in far suburbs like Beachwood and Westlake to buy clothes, though the aforementioned independents are beginning to fill some of the gap.

Recent years have seen an improvement in city residents' access to useful if fascistic big box stores like Target and Home Depot. Steelyard Commons, just south of Downtown, has a wide array of these stores, and many of these are duplicated along W. 117th Street.

If you're trying to avoid the malls and the deep suburbs, try these places, arranged by category; those marked with an asterisk are independently and/or locally owned:

Grocery with Full Produce Section
• West Side Market*, 1979 W. 25th St.
• Dave's Supermarket* (locations in Asiatown, North Collinwood,
  Shaker Square, Cleveland Heights, Ohio City, Clark-Metro, Slavic Village)
• Giant Eagle (locations in Shaker Square/Buckeye, Westown, West Park and
  Lakewood, and near Old Brooklyn)
• Nature's Bin*, 18120 Sloane Ave., Lakewood
• Zagara's Market*, 1940 Lee Rd., Cleveland Heights
• Marc's* (locations in West Park, Westown, Cleveland Heights and Lakewood)

Imported/Ethnic Grocery with Some Produce
• Asian Town Centre*, 3820 Superior Ave. (Asian)
• Tink Holl*, 1735 E. 36th St. (Asian)
• Park 2 Shop*, 1580 E. 30th St. (Asian)
• Halal Meats*, 9418 Detroit Ave. (Middle Eastern)
• Aladdin's*, 1301 Carnegie Ave. (Middle Eastern)
• Gallucci's Italian Foods*, 6610 Euclid Ave. (Italian)
• Murray Hill Market*, 2072 Murray Hill Rd. (Italian)
• Gentile's*, 4464 Broadview Rd. (Italian)
• Hansa Haus*, 2717 Lorain Ave. (German)
• Jasmine Bakery*, 16700 Lorain Ave. (Middle Eastern)
• Supermercado Rico*, 4706 Lorain Ave. (Latino)
• La Plaza Supermarket*, 13609 Lakewood Heights Blvd., Lakewood (Latino)

Bread Bakeries

- Various locations inside the West Side Market, 1979 W. 25th St.
- On the Rise*, 3471 Fairmount Blvd., Cleveland Heights
- Stone Oven*, 2267 Lee Rd., Cleveland Heights; 1301 E. 9th St. inside the Galleria Food Court
- Zoss the Baker*, 12397 Cedar Rd., Cleveland Heights
- Breadsmith*, 18101 Detroit Rd., Lakewood

Pastries & Sweets

- Various locations inside the West Side Market, 1979 W. 25th St.
- Gypsy Beans & Baking Co.*, 6425 Detroit Ave.
- A Cookie & A Cupcake*, 2173 Professor St.
- Lilly Handmade Chocolate*, 761 Starkweather Ave.
- Sweet Moses*, 6800 Detroit Ave.
- Ohio City Ice Cream*, 4401 Bridge Ave.
- Lucky's Café*, 777 Starkweather Ave.
- Corbo's*, 12210 Mayfield Rd.
- Presti's*, 12101 Mayfield Rd.
- Baker's Bakery*, 3550 W. 105th St.
- Azucar Bakery*, 6516 Lorain Ave.
- Bonbon Pastry & Cafe*, 2549 Lorain Ave.
- Maggie's Vegan Bakery*, 1830 W. 25th St.

Clothing

- Dredger's Union*, 2043 E. 4th St. (men's and women's)
- Banyan Tree*, 2242 Professor St. (mostly women's, some men's)
- TurnStyle*, 6505 Detroit Ave. (women's)
- Evie Lou*, 2153 Literary Ave. (women's)
- Powter Puff Boutique*, 2671 W. 14th St. (women's)
- Native Cleveland*, 15813 Waterloo Rd. (local interest T-shirts)
- C9 Boutique*, 15613 Waterloo Rd. (men's and women's)
- Avalon Exchange*, 1798 Coventry Rd. (thrift)
- Blush Boutique*, 1783 Coventry Rd. (locally designed women's)
- Heart & Sole Sneakers*, 1781 Coventry Rd. (shoes)
- Next*, 1796 Coventry and inside Tower City (urban active)
- Revive*, 2248 Lee Rd. (fair trade)
- Frog's Legs*, 12807 Larchmere Blvd. (men's and women's)

- Christophier*, 9308 Clifton Blvd. (men's formal and business)
- Geiger's Clothing & Sports*, 14710 Detroit Ave., Lakewood (men's)
- American Apparel, 1782 Coventry Rd., Cleveland Heights (men's and women's)
- Tower City Center mall also has chains like Brooks Brothers, Victoria's Secret and Jones New York.

Music
- Bent Crayon*, 11600 Detroit Ave.
- Music Saves*, 15801 Waterloo Rd.
- Loop*, 2180 W. 11th St.
- fye, Tower City Center
- Best Buy, 3506 Steelyard Dr.
- The Exchange*, 15006 Detroit Ave., Lakewood

Books
- Visible Voice*, 1023 Kenilworth Ave.
- Horizontal Books*, 1921 W. 25th St.
- Loganberry Books*, 13015 Larchmere Blvd.
- Carol & John's Comic Shop*, 17462 Lorain Ave.
- Barnes & Noble College Store, 2020 Euclid Ave.
- Appletree Books*, 12419 Cedar Rd., Cleveland Heights
- Mac's Backs Books*, 1820 Coventry Rd., Cleveland Heights

Electronics
- Radio Shack, 520 Euclid Ave.
- Best Buy, 3605 Steelyard Dr.

Home Furnishings
- Room Service*, 2078 W. 25th St.
- Duo Home*, 6507 Detroit Ave.
- Surroundings Home Décor*, 850 W. St. Clair Ave.
- Reincarnation*, 7810 Lorain Ave.
- Schindler's Fabrics & Upholstery*, 9933 Lorain Ave.
- Futon Factory*, 2400 Superior Ave.
- Norton Furniture*, 2106 Payne Ave.

Bicycle Shops & Repair
- Joy Machines*, 1836 W. 25th St.
- Fridrich Bicycle*, 3800 Lorain Ave.
- Blazing Saddles*, 7427 Detroit Ave.
- Blue Sky Bicycle Shop*, 565 E. 185th St.
- Shaker Cycle*, 2389 W. 5th St.
- Lorain Triskett Cycle & Fitness*, 15718 Lorain Ave.
- Spin*, 14515 Madison Ave., Lakewood
- Cain Park Bicycle*, 1904 Lee Rd., Cleveland Heights

Hardware, Building Supply, etc.
- Cleveland Lumber*, 9410 Madison Ave.
- West End Lumber*, 4520 W. 130th St.
- Castro & Sons Hardware*, 4313 Clark Ave.
- South Hills Hardware*, 224 Old Brookpark Rd.
- Heights Hardware*, 1792 Coventry Rd., Cleveland Heights
- Lakewood Hardware*, 16608 Madison Ave., Lakewood

Craft Supply
- Pat Catan's*, 12775 Berea Rd.

Big Box
- Best Buy, 3605 Steelyard Dr.
- Target, 3535 Steelyard Dr.; 3100 W. 117th St.
- Wal-Mart, 3400 Steelyard Dr.
- Staples, 3373 Steelyard Dr.; 2150 W. 117th St.
- Home Depot, 3355 Steelyard Dr.; 11901 Berea Rd.
- A.J. Wright, 10756 Lorain Ave.

THE WEATHER

Clevelanders never get tired of complaining about winter weather. Perhaps the only more popular point of commiseration is the pathetic state of the Browns and the Indians (and now, in LeBron James' absence, the Cavs).

So how bad, really, is winter in Cleveland? The answer, of course, depends on your personality and the type of climate you're accustomed to. People who've relocated here from the West or the South – where winters are sunny and sometimes even warm – tend to have the most trouble. Average high temperatures from December through February range from 34 to 38 degrees, and the skies are often grey. Cleveland ranks among the top 10 cities in the U.S. for number of cloudy or overcast days, according to the National Oceanic and Atmospheric Administration – but we're not as cloudy as Portland, Ore. or Seattle.

The relative lack of activity and early nightfall in winter (the sun sets as early as 5 p.m. around the winter solstice) can also be difficult for extroverts. The city enters a hibernation period from about November to March, broken only by the winter holidays. There are few parties and few large-scale events of the type you'll find every weekend in summer.

People who have to drive long distances to work also struggle in the winter, because Cleveland gets a lot of snow (an average of 57 inches per year). In general, the East Side of the city and its eastern suburbs get more snowfall than the West, due to a phenomenon known locally as the "lake effect" (as in "lake effect snow"). Weather systems moving east over Lake Erie from the north pick up moisture, which mixes with cold air and turns into snow. Or something like that.

On the other hand, people from other parts of the Midwest or Northeast likely won't find the transition so tough. Cleveland's winter temperatures are a few degrees warmer, on average, than in cities like Chicago, Toronto and Minneapolis. And introverts may welcome winter's built-in solitude and quiet.

Meanwhile, more and more Clevelanders are discovering that outdoor sports and activities can be an antidote to cabin fever. Cross country skiing is becoming a particular favorite. If you own your own skis, you can take to the trails at any of the Cleveland MetroParks, Shaker Lakes or in the Cuyahoga Valley National Park. Chapin Forest, 10090 Chillocothe Rd. in Kirtland, rents skis for about $5 an hour.

Other popular winter activities are tobogganing (available at the MetroParks' Mill Stream Run Reservation, 16200 Valley Parkway, Strongsville); sledding (available anywhere there's a hill – for example at Edgewater Park); and ice skating (there are rinks at the city's Halloran Park at 3550 W. 117th St. and at Wade Oval in University Circle). If you're a jogger, there are few days when it's too cold or icy to squeeze in a few miles.

If you're not a fan of winter, and have the financial means, a trip South can also be a lifesaver. Florida is probably the most population destination for the non-winter-inclined. But you can also find surprisingly affordable and direct flights to Puerto Rico and Mexico.

Overshadowed by all the belly-aching about winter, of course, is the pleasantness of the other three seasons. Fall and spring are brief but glorious, with temperatures in the 60s and 70s and low humidity. Street trees and forested areas in parks light up with color in fall, and spring's buds are equally beautiful.

Summer in Cleveland, meanwhile, is one long party. From June through August, there are parties and events just about every night – and dozens on the weekends – as people rush to take advantage of the warm weather and long nights. (The sun doesn't set until 9 p.m. for much of June and July.) The busy-ness of the season can feel almost Bacchanalian, as the entire city releases pent up energy from the quiet winter.

Summer weather is hot and the air becomes soupy with humidity. Transplants from desert cities in the Southwest and West may find the humidity as shocking as the winter cold. But again, Cleveland fares well in comparison to other cities of the Midwest and East Coast. Temperatures are generally at least five degrees cooler than in steamy New York City or Washington, D.C., for example, and much lower than any place in the Southeast. Many Cleveland houses don't even have air conditioning, since temperatures become unpleasantly hot only a few days out of every year. Average high temperatures in June, July and August are 79, 83 and 81, respectively. Cooler weather prevails by late September.

CRIME & SAFETY

Taken at face value, Cleveland's crime rates can be troubling. Per capita rates of violent and property crime, as measured by the FBI, are often two or three times higher than in the U.S. as a whole. Many other U.S. cities, including Chicago, Miami, Minneapolis, Atlanta and Philadelphia, are in the same boat.

The good news is that Cleveland today is much safer than it was 20 years ago. In the city proper, incidents of both violent crime and property crime fell 35 percent between 1990

and 2010, according to the Cleveland Police Department. This mirrors a national trend that many crime experts attribute to the lessening of the crack epidemic since the early 1990s.

Rates of crime – in Cleveland as elsewhere – correlate with socioeconomic factors such as poverty, transience and educational attainment. As it has sought to redefine itself in the post-industrial era, Cleveland has had high numbers of people fitting all of those descriptors. Many turn to crime out of desperation.

The chances that you'll be a victim of a violent crime in Cleveland are very small. In 2010, for example, the Cleveland Police Department reported about 6,000 incidents of homicide, rape, robbery and felonious assault. Property crimes were more common, with about 32,000 incidents of burglary, theft, vehicle theft and arson. But viewed in the context of a city of about 400,000 people, these numbers make clear that the vast majority of Clevelanders are unaffected. I'm knocking on wood as I write this, but in the six years since I moved back to Cleveland – always living in the city proper – the only thing I've had go wrong was that my bike was stolen once when I didn't lock it.

The Nature Center at Shaker Lakes day 44/100

More important than numbers, though, are people's perceptions of safety. Many Northeast Ohio residents who lived through the city's darkest period – from the 1960s through the 1980s – remain more cautious and fearful of crime in the city than reality may warrant. You'll encounter many suburbanites above the age of 50, for example, who view a visit to Downtown as a death wish. Some younger suburbanites have inherited their parents' and grandparents' views. Don't let them scare you.

Transplants from bigger cities may find Cleveland's sidewalks eerily deserted and unsafe-feeling, even if there's no real threat. Especially during the colder months when many Clevelanders huddle up on their sofas, you may find yourself one of the few people on the sidewalk in Downtown and many neighborhoods. Women, in particular, report feeling unsafe walking in Downtown Cleveland and closer-in neighborhoods at night. One hopes this will improve as Downtown and neighborhood revitalization efforts continue, but in the meantime the Downtown Cleveland Alliance offers an escort service if you find yourself feeling unsafe.

Aggressive panhandling is another phenomenon that troubles a lot of folks even though it doesn't usually pose a safety threat. Until recently, panhandlers were especially prevalent Downtown and on W. 25th Street in Ohio City. To deal with the problem, both neighborhoods now have special improvement districts with ambassadors who direct panhandlers to social service agencies that help them find food, shelter and counseling.

A few simple measures can help prevent property crime. Keep your doors locked and windows closed, for example, when you're not home. If you have a house, keep a porch light on at night. Install a security system. When you're out of town, ask a neighbor to keep an eye on your place. Keep your car locked. Lock your bike. In both your car and house, place all valuables out of sight. (Examples: Don't leave your laptop – or even loose change – on the passenger seat of your car, and think twice about installing your new large-screen TV in a place where everyone can see it from the sidewalk.)

A word of warning: In a couple of the neighborhoods where I've lived, I've ended up on resident email lists – often delivered via something like Yahoo! Groups. These lists are well-meaning but often devolve into obsessive discussions of petty property crimes and hearsay. They tend to spark fear rather than community cohesion or productive solutions. Avoid them, and instead attend local block club meetings, which tend to be more positive. You can find out about these from your local community development corporation.

FRIENDS & RELATIONSHIPS

When I decided to move back to Cleveland a few years back, the biggest question on my mind was: Will I be able to meet people?

I'm happy to say that I found meeting people to be a breeze. Of course, I had a leg up: I was starting a degree program. Every day, I sat in classes with people who had similar interests, and were of a similar age. Some of them became close friends.

But I also met plenty of people outside of class. I met them at coffee shops. I met them at summer events. I met them through jobs. I met them at public lectures. I didn't have to try hard, or "be outgoing": I was simply getting involved in things that naturally interested me.

Contrary to all my fears, I found meeting people in Cleveland to be even easier than it had been in New York. I have a theory about this. Because Cleveland is a relatively small city, it's easy to "find your people" here. The degrees of separation are smaller, so it doesn't take long to get plugged into networks of people with similar interests ("affinity groups," in marketing terms).

Now, I'm not saying everyone who moves here will have the same experience. I've heard from a few people who have struggled to find a place for themselves in Cleveland. They find that many Clevelanders – especially the ones who have lived here their whole lives – have had the same friends since high school, and aren't looking for new ones. Younger, single transplants may find that even coworkers their own age have long since settled in the far suburbs with a spouse and kids. There's no chance of grabbing drinks or coffee after work with these folks because they need to rush out right at 5 p.m. to pick up Olivia and Ethan from daycare.

These are valid complaints. Cleveland isn't a city where it's assumed that you've come from elsewhere and there's a collective sense of "starting anew."

But I'm going to say something provocative: I think people who have a hard time making friends in Cleveland aren't trying very hard. Maybe they didn't want to come here in the first place, and they're looking to get out as fast as they can. Or maybe they hate their jobs. So they don't invest in finding friends. And when they don't find any, that gives them one more reason to pack up and move on.

What about dating? Again, there are as many experiences with this as there are Clevelanders. But in general, Cleveland is a relationship-oriented town. I haven't done any empirical studies, but my observation is that Clevelanders tend to settle down with serious partners earlier and more readily than do their counterparts on the coasts. On the plus side, you may find Clevelanders' openness to commitment refreshing – especially if you're exhausted by the frenetic dating circuit of bigger cities.

Online dating is less popular in Cleveland than in many other cities. Part of this is a function of Cleveland's relatively small size. Start trolling online dating sites and you're likely to see some coworkers or friends – always an awkward experience. I do know people who have met online, though, so it's worth a shot.

Networking and social opportunities for particular groups include: The Young Latino Network, www.younglatinonetwork.org; The 20-30 Club, www.cleveland2030.org; The Cleveland Professionals Group, www.clevelandprofessionals.com; Plexus, a networking group for gay professionals, www.thinkplexus.org; the Cleveland Hiking Club, www.clevelandhikingclub.org; and many others. Many individual professions and universities also have local networking groups. A quick Google search will unearth them.

In general, if you want to meet people, put yourself in the thick of things. Live in an urban neighborhood with lots of stuff to do and places to hang out. Your chances of making new acquaintances will skyrocket, because there will be so many chances for accidental encounters. That's part of the beauty of city life.

GAY LIFE IN CLEVELAND

Like many states, Ohio has an amendment to its state constitution defining marriage as between a man and a woman. The amendment also forbids any parallel system (such as civil unions) that "approximate" marriage. That, along with the state's generally conservative politics, has given the state a reputation for being anti-gay. Many gay people have fled to friendlier pastures. (Gay adoption is legal, however.)

Yet the city of Cleveland and some inner-ring suburbs have done their best to be welcoming even within the straightjacket of state policy. The city started a domestic partner registry in 2010, and Cleveland Heights has one too. (Neither registry conveys legal rights to gay couples; they're largely symbolic.) Positively Cleveland – the city's tourism bureau that sounds like an HIV-prevention program but isn't – runs a program called Cleveland Plus LGBT that markets the city to gay visitors.

The Lesbian and Gay Center of Cleveland (6600 Detroit Ave.) has an active slate of events, support groups and youth outreach programs. There's also a gay chamber of commerce, called Plexus.

And, in a coup for the local gay community, Cleveland will host the Gay Games in 2014. The Games' selection committee chose Cleveland because of the city's progressive policies, but also because the committee wanted to heighten awareness of gay issues outside the East and West coasts. One of the games' top judges was so impressed with Cleveland's culture and affordability that he bought a condo in Ohio City.

If you're political, the Cleveland Stonewall Democrats wields some influence over local Democratic candidates. The local chapter of the Human Rights Campaign, meanwhile, has undertaken the huge task of trying to change state policy about gay marriage.

Like their straight counterparts, Cleveland gays tend to be a couple-oriented lot. The social scene doesn't hold a candle to places like New York, Chicago or Toronto. The number of bars and clubs is small and continues to fall, probably due at least in part to the growth of online dating. The silver lining is that the places that remain have become more diverse. People of all genders and races now converge at popular spots like Union Station in Ohio City and Twist in Edgewater, though there are other bars scattered around the West Side. There's also a popular and fun monthly gay gathering, called G2H2 (Gay Guy/Girl Happy Hour), that alights at a different bar each month. Check www.g2h2.com.

EDUCATION IN CLEVELAND

Like many older cities in the East and Midwest, Cleveland has troubled public schools. The problem began after World War II, with the flight of middle-class and affluent families to the suburbs. With those families went valuable tax revenue, leaving urban schools with dwindling resources.

In the late 1970s, a court decision required the city school district to institute mandatory cross-town busing. Busing was supposed to end de facto racial segregation by shuttling kids between the mostly black East Side and the mostly white West Side. But the program backfired for a mix of social, economic and logistical reasons, speeding the flight of more affluent families to suburbs where busing wasn't required. The tax base eroded further, and Cleveland's public schools reached new levels of financial hardship. Busing ended in 1996, too late to stop the bleeding.

The Cleveland Metropolitan School District is now a fraction of its peak size. Enrollment at the city's public school population dropped to less than 50,000 in 2010, from 135,000 in 1960.

The Cinematheque at the Cleveland Institute of Art

day 96/100

Yet there's also a hopeful story behind that decline. Part of the reason the public schools have lost students is that – thanks to charter schools and vouchers – city parents now have a greater range of education options than ever before. By many accounts, the Cleveland public schools have countered this increased competition by becoming more creative and effective in their own handling of primary and secondary education.

The Interactive Local Report Card program of the Ohio Department of Education ranks a growing number of schools in Cleveland as "Excellent," on par with the best suburban schools. These include Tremont Montessori (K-8), The Cleveland School of the Arts (K-12) and John Hay High School (9-12), which offers a general program as well as specialty programs in Science & Medicine and Architecture & Design. Cleveland State University helped found the new Campus International School (3000 Euclid Ave.), which will eventually expand to K-12.

Some schools have become well-integrated, while others remain predominantly single-race. The Cleveland School of the Arts High School in University Circle, for example, is 90% percent black, while Benjamin Franklin Elementary in Old Brooklyn is 87% white. (Both schools, incidentally, are rated "Excellent.") In cases such as these, parents will need to ask themselves whether they are comfortable with their children being part of either a large majority or a small minority. Demographic information is available on the state's interactive local report cards.

Today, parents in the City of Cleveland have four basic options for educating their children: general public schools, specialty public schools, charter schools and private schools. Most schools in Cleveland are either primary (kindergarten through eighth grade) or secondary (high school).

General public schools. These are the schools your child will attend if you make no other choice. They operate by neighborhood, or "catchment area," meaning that the school your child will attend is based on your address. You can request that your child attend a general public school in another catchment area, but the district will grant the request only if there's space after all the neighborhood students have enrolled.

Specialty public schools. Partly in response to increased competition from charters, the Cleveland Municipal School District operates several primary and secondary schools. These usually have a curriculum focused around specific topic areas – the arts or science and technology, for example – or are single-sex, or have an institutional affiliation. The district maintains a list of specialty schools on its Web site. Examples include The Cleveland School of the Arts (K-8 and high school at separate buildings); Campus International School (affiliated with Cleveland State University, currently K-3 but expected to grow to K-12); and several single-sex schools.

Charter schools. The State of Ohio allowed the creation of charter schools – which are publicly funded but privately operated – starting in 1997. There are now dozens in the City of Cleveland, with a total enrollment of about 14,000. These, too, often have a specialty focus or a novel approach to curriculum and learning. Parents do not pay tuition for charter schools; the State of Ohio provides all funding. Many charter schools haven't lasted long, but a few have been big successes. Perhaps the best known are E-Prep, in Asiatown, and The Integenerational School, on Shaker Square. E-Prep, short for Entrepreneurship Preparatory School, teaches kids entrepreneurship skills in addition to a general curriculum; The Intergenerational School clusters kids across skill levels, rather than age groups, and sets them up with adult mentors. Both schools operate under the well-regarded Breakthrough Charter Schools umbrella. In 2011, parents on the city's Near West Side organized to lure a new branch of the Intergenerational School to their neighborhood. The Near West Intergenerational School opened in Fall 2011 inside Garrett Morgan School of Science in Ohio City.

Private schools. Most of the private schools in Cleveland proper are Catholic, with a few exceptions – Birchwood School (K-8) in West Park, for example, and Montessori High School at University Circle. You can find a list of Catholic schools in Cleveland on the website of the Catholic Diocese of Cleveland's Office of Catholic Education. Some of the better-known Catholic schools in Cleveland include Urban Community School (K-8) in Ohio City; St. Ignatius High School (boys only) in Ohio City; St. Joseph Academy High School (girls) in West Park; and Cleveland Central Catholic High School (co-ed) in Slavic Village. You can find a list of non-parochial private schools in Cleveland and its suburbs on the Web site of the Cleveland Council of Independent Schools. Private schools charge tuition, but some are enrolled in the state-administered Cleveland school voucher program, which pays up to $3,450 in tuition for K-12 private schools based on family income. Even with this program, parents pay at least 10 percent of the total tuition. About 5,300 students in Cleveland use the voucher program. Some private schools also offer their own scholarship programs.

Given the range of choices, and the potential that your kid may attend school in a neighborhood (or even a suburb) far from where you live, transportation can be an important consideration. If you choose a general or specialty public school farther than two miles from your home, CMSD will provide free bus transportation. Some private schools also offer buses for far-flung students.

Let's say you're a parent of elementary school-age kids, and you've just moved to town. What's the process for getting your kids enrolled in school?

First, research your choices. Check out the Web site of CMSD to find out about the district's general and specialty schools. Ask neighbors about charter schools, and, if you're interested, look at the Web sites of the Office of Catholic Education, the Council of Independent Schools (listed above) or Google "Montessori schools Cleveland."

After you've made a list of schools you like, you can check how public and charter schools rate on the state's interactive local report card. On the home page, click on "Find a School Building Report." The report cards contain valuable information about overall student performance, and assign each school a ranking from Excellent to Academic Emergency. (Of course, these "grades" are generalized, and can't predict the individual performance of your child.) The state does not rate private schools.

Most importantly, call ahead to schedule visits at the schools that interest you; phone numbers are readily available online.

If you decide to pursue a general or specialty CMSD school, fill out the open enrollment form at the Office of Student Assignments, 1440 Lakeside Avenue, 216-523-6347. CMSD assigns students to specialty schools on a lottery system, where parents list their first, second and third choices.

If you decide to pursue a charter school or a private school, you'll work through the individual school's admissions department. Private schools will guide you through the voucher application process.

Parents interested in private schools should also keep in mind that the cost of private education may be wholly or partly offset by tax savings from living in the City of Cleveland. The city's property taxes are lower than just about any suburb's. They're even cheaper (or nonexistent) if you're living in a tax-abated property (see box, p. 83). Those savings could go toward private school tuition, or even to help save for college.

AFTERWORD

———

Part of what makes cities exciting is how quickly they change and evolve. Just since I wrote the main text for this book in Summer 2011, new stores and restaurants have opened; others have closed. Cleveland's many nonprofits and civic organizations have begun new, promising initiatives to lead the city in positive directions.

Every day, there is a New Cleveland. And every day — whether we've lived here for years or just relocated — each one of us can be New to Cleveland. If there's anything that Julia and I hope this book has inspired you to do, it's to go out, explore, appreciate, learn.

Cleveland is waiting for you.

ACKNOWLEDGMENTS

Justin

First, thanks to Dan – for everything. Thanks to the people who gave their time to read the text when it was still in draft, including Tracey Kastelic, Dan McDonald, and Lora DiFranco. For their enthusiastic feedback, I owe a special debt of gratitude to the Wimbiscus family: Joel and Molly Wimbiscus and Laura Wimbiscus Yoon. Joel, thank you for your ongoing thoughts and for loving Cleveland even more than I do. Thanks to Emilio DiSabato, JP Kilroy, Cory Riordan and Christopher Lohr for showing me your parts of the city and sharing your stories. A huge thank you to Eric Wobser at Ohio City Inc. for believing in this project and for being such a great friend. Next Halloweekend is on me. Thanks to Piet Van Lier for sharing his knowledge of the school system. Thanks to Lee Zelenak at Kiddo for designing such a beautiful book, and to Danielle DeBoe and Brian Jasinski for introducing me to him. To Julia, thank you for your incredible drawings, your creativity and your easy way of being yourself. You are an inspiration. Thanks to my parents for encouraging me to make books when I was a kid. And thank you, Becca, for being my light.

Julia

Thanks to Charity Ewanko at iheartcleveland, Connie Schultz and Michael K. McIntyre at the Plain Dealer, Dave DeOreo and Dee Perry at NPR, Jenn Holton at Cleveland Magazine, and Rory O'Connor at Shaker Life for finding the blog newsworthy!
And thank you Margaret and Reena at the Rock Hall and Allison and Ksenia at Cain Park for reaching out and generously giving me your time - I appreciated every minute of it. Thank you also to every kind person that wrote me an email out of the blue just to tell me what you thought about the blog. You quickly became the audience I was drawing for. Justin, I knew from the moment I read your text that I wanted to work with you! It's been nothing but great, and I can't wait to read more of your books.And last but not least, T.G, J.P, E.G and L.K - my Cleveland memories will always be anchored to you.

The Chess Players

day 9/100

JUSTIN GLANVILLE

Justin Glanville grew up in the suburbs of Cleveland and now lives on the city's near West Side. He worked as a reporter for The Associated Press in New York before returning to Cleveland in 2005. He studied Classics at Grinnell College in Iowa and has a master's degree in urban planning, design and development from Cleveland State University. He has worked for the Cleveland nonprofits ParkWorks and Cleveland Public Art. For his writing, he is recipient of a 2012 Creative Workforce Fellowship from the Community Partnership for Arts and Culture.

JULIA KUO

Julia Kuo is a Taiwanese American freelance illustrator. She grew up in Los Angeles and attended Washington University in St. Louis for illustration and marketing. Following graduation, she moved to Cleveland in 2007 to design greeting cards at American Greetings. Since then Julia has taken the full-time plunge, working from coffee shops around the city for a variety of clients. She illustrates for newspaper and magazines, children's books, album covers and concert posters, and more. You can see her work at juliakuo.com and thenimbusfactory.com.

The Hung house

day 49/100